INSIGHT AND ACTION:

THE ROLE OF THE UNCONSCIOUS IN CRISIS
FROM THE PERSONAL TO INTERNATIONAL LEVELS

Barry Austin Goodfield, PhD

Edited by William Noel Munday

UNIVERSITY OF WESTMINSTER PRESS, LONDON

Distributed by MARYLEBONE BOOKS, University of Westminster
35 Marylebone Road, London NW1 5LS

First published in 1999 by the
University of Westminster Press
309 Regent Street, London W1R 8AL, United Kingdom

Insight and Action:
The role of the unconscious in crisis
from the personal to international levels

British Library Cataloguing in Publication Data
A catalogue record for this book is available from the
British Library

ISBN 1 85919 106 1

Design and Production Editor: Christine Lewsey, Marketing and Development Office,
University of Westminster, 115 New Cavendish Street, London W1M 8JS UK

Cover Design: Sian Cardy

Typesetting: Alyson Hall, MZZ Typesetters

Set in Bookman 9.5pt type on 12pt leading and Argo

Printer: Linneys Four Colour

FOR
DORI, ERIC AND JANE FELICE

INSIGHT AND ACTION:

THE ROLE OF THE UNCONSCIOUS IN CRISIS
FROM THE PERSONAL TO INTERNATIONAL LEVELS

Edited by

William Noel Munday

CONTENTS

FORWARD

This book is about computers, but not the sort of artificial, often maddening, man-made device that has come to dominate the end of our millennium. Doctor Goodfield has written about the programmed responses of the human brain and all of the soft hardware that goes with it.

Combining his intuitive skills with psychological research, Goodfield has learned to read responses from the brain and body, which in certain ways can be as precise as information stored on a microchip. And yet it is enriched by emotions and feelings that cannot be defined in anyone's language.

As a result, this work is as new as the space age and as old as human beings. It probes the basic questions of individual behavior and communication among individuals. Doctor Goodfield is at once a specialist in describing the obvious and in finding hidden clues toward unveiling what may seem to be the unfathomable.

While we may receive information from many sources, we often overlook the most important one: direct messages sent to us by signals people do not even realize they are sending. At the same time, we transmit these signals to others, unequally unaware of what we are unconsciously saying. These "non-verbal leaks," unfiltered are vital to real understanding, whether in a personal relationship or in summit-level crisis negotiation.

Goodfield's work has made this arcane human language accessible to those who can put it to essential use: in diplomacy, in communications, in corporate negotiation, in crisis management, in day-to-day life. It enables the observant to recognize, analyze, understand and use non-verbal information to diagnose situations.

Clearly, information is crucial to our understanding of all situations. And the non-verbal leak unblocks the conscious barriers of those who seek to dissimulate and delude. Especially in international relations where secrecy and double dealing are common coin, the non-verbal leak is a valuable tool.

Even in negotiation in the best of faith, cross-cultural differences among negotiators create ambiguity. The stress of negotiating in crisis narrows down the few insights we might have, particularly at times when human lives and national integrity are at stake.

Yet while people are different by character and culture, the signals they transmit are universal. And this is what Goodfield brings to us. He brings us a reliable lingua franca, without words to lead us astray.

At a time in our global development when so much inanimate data can be committed to hard drives, when we can e-mail complex graphics from Timbuktu to the depths of Patagonia, we can now do something similar with the bytes and bits of inner human responses.

Goodfield's work can only help us all.

Paul W. Meerts, M.A.
Consultant in Diplomatic Training and Deputy Director of the
Netherlands Institute of International relations "Clingendael"

PREFACE

This book is based on a simple belief that winning depends on a decision made prior to victory. And victory, in this context, means a win-win result of mutual success in communication and objectives.

Essential to victory is skill in reading the non-verbal leaks of those with whom you negotiate.

Too many agreements fail simply because they are not based on clear interpretations of feelings and facts. When conscious and unconscious information is overlooked, an accord is likely to unravel. When this crucial data forms the basis for agreement, a natural balance all but ensures success.

Success depends upon winning strategies and the personal determination to pay a price greater than that paid by others. The non-verbal leak is the key to determining the real prices at issue.

This is a new work, but it has developed over the years and is rooted deeply in the basics of psychology. If crisis and conflict are to be overcome, they require specific skills and tools. This book is intended to help you with the three essential strategies: to organize, to fight and win.

The greater goal of life is balance, and the Goodfield Method seeks to bring the discord of crisis and conflict into that balance. It is a systematic, body-oriented analysis of an individual's consciously and unconsciously generated communications. The elements of this method have been tested over time.

Taken together, they add up to what I believe are reliable means to observe and evaluate a person's behavior. This allows negotiations to be more productive, questions to be clearer, confidence to be increased and differences to become less important.

I welcome you along on an adventure that has occupied more than thirty years of my life, an exploration of insights and actions toward the heart of the human condition.

Barry Austin Goodfield

ACKNOWLEDGEMENTS

Writing a book is like living a life, a daily confrontation with one's self. I have been extremely lucky to have good friends around me to help. Bill Munday, along with his giving wife, Carolyn, devoted uncounted days to this project. Bill was there when it all started and will surely be there at the end. This would not have happened without him.

In the beginning there was Mort. Mort Rosenblum, award-winning journalist, world roamer, and life-long friend, always found time to help straighten my bent prose. Many of the adventures in this book might have turned out differently if he had not been there.

Some of my best friends are in a group we call the Eagles, because we try to fly high, straight and alone. From time to time we meet to make a good life better. They are always there in a crisis.

A special thanks goes to Elly Bakx, whose energy and skill were essential to putting together the manuscript.

I've lived much of my life on the road; routinely people who know me add, "How long are you staying?" to hello. When you go somewhere, you leave somewhere else. To family members left behind, who have nonetheless offered love and understanding when leaving, thanks for the love and understanding. I am deeply grateful. To my wonderful wife, Dori, and our little girl, Jane Felice: I'll try to get it right this time.

INTRODUCTION

The goal of life is balance, and the Goodfield Method of conflict resolution and crisis management brings that balance into the arena of discord. It is a systematic, body-oriented analysis of one's consciously and unconsciously generated communications.

Some of the elements of the method may seem, initially, to be like magic; but they have been tested over time, scientifically, and proven to be paths to the unconscious processes, so that people's behaviors can be understood and evaluated by laypersons. With this method, we see the non-verbal behaviors as signs and signals reflecting the unconscious forces that drive and direct our lives. Negotiations become more productive, questions are more clarified, confidence is increased, and differences become less important.

I welcome you as you join me in a trek that has charged more than thirty years of my life, as we explore what I consider to be the most fascinating adventure of them all: the study of our insights and our actions. I hope this book will help to illuminate those areas where light is most needed: on the human condition, man's needs and his suffering.

AN OVERVIEW OF THE GOODFIELD METHOD

All psychological systems are based in some philosophical belief or beliefs about the nature of man. Carl Rogers believed that man is intrinsically good and that, if he were allowed to "be himself," he would be noble. John B. Watson and, later, B.F. Skinner developed the notion that we learn to be whom we are, that we are blank slates waiting to become what the chalk of living designs us to be.

The various schools are all well known. As college freshmen we studied psychoanalytical psychology, social psychology, behaviorism, perhaps even industrial psychology and all the rest; and it was expected that we would choose one or another of them as the basis of our life's work. Most of us did just that and we called ourselves by the choices we made: we were Jungian or Gestaltists or whatever.

Dr. Goodfield, however, chose his own path. He was suspicious of the diagnostic labels of which members of our field are so fond. He granted the psychiatrist his area, the psychoses, and allowed as how treatment by medication was obviously appropriate; but he considered the neuroses to be a different matter.

As he worked, in his practice, with people whose actions and interactions were so self-defeating, so out of character, that both he and the client were often at a loss to explain them, he began to understand neurotic behaviors as being the products of incongruence between the individual's self and his self-concept. He began to see, over time, that many people were locked into problem solving strategies that were not only ineffective, but that exacerbated their difficulties. From where did these strategies come?

He reasoned that, at some point in the client's life, probably at a very early age, he made a decision about how to deal with what he believed was some balance threatening, or even life-threatening, event and, when the strategy worked, or so he thought, he adopted it. As he grew older, his world and its challenges changed completely, but he continued to apply the strategy that sprang from the old decision regardless of its shortcomings. Working with these old self-defeating decisions and helping people discover more effective life strategies has been Dr. Goodfield's life's work.

Bill Munday

1 THE THEORETICAL PLACEMENT OF THE GOODFIELD METHOD AS IT RELATES TO OTHER BEHAVIORAL DISCIPLINES

The reader, as he researches the history of the development of psychological thought, will find no discovery more fascinating than the Freudian slip, the inadvertent introduction of a wrong word or phrase, irrelevant to the rest of the sentence, or radically changing its meaning, contrary to the conscious intention of the speaker, but interpreted by psychoanalysts as the expression of a repressed wish.

An extraordinarily innovative and inquisitive man, Freud reasoned that these slips revealed hidden dimensions of the personality that he called the unconscious. He saw that we leak our hidden thoughts on a level below our awareness, and he wrote on this topic as early as 1905:

> "When I set myself the task of bringing to light what human beings keep hidden within them, not by the compelling power of hypnosis, but by observing what they say and what they show, I thought the task was a harder one than it really is. He who has eyes to see and ears to hear may convince himself that no mortal can keep a secret. If his lips are sealed, he chatters with his fingertips; betrayal oozes out of him at every pore, and thus the task of making conscious the most hidden recesses of the mind is one which it is quite possible to accomplish."

It is well known, also, that Freud believed that much of one's personality is formed in his very early years.

Just when we start to record impressions of the world around us, however, is a matter of considerable debate. Still, Freud's postulation holds great merit; all stories have beginnings and, for the human being's, they begin in the mother who is, in all cases, a woman. For some individuals, this fact forms the basis for later difficulties. R.D. Laing once remarked that he reckoned that the first trauma begins with conception shock.

The world's recognized authority on general semantics and communications theory, the late Dr. S.I. Hayakawa shared with Dr. Carl Rogers, founder of Rogerian Therapy, beliefs about congruence and incongruence between verbal and non-verbal language.

Hayakawa generated the theory of the symbolic self and Rogers developed the theory of the self-concept.

They believed that there were two basic aspects of the personality. First, there is the self, the sum total of the individual on all levels, biologically, physically, psychologically, educationally, etc. The self-concept, on the other hand, is a conglomerate made up of those value judgments we make about ourselves: "I am an educated person, a fine arts lover, and I am capable of great passion." When the self and the self-concept are incongruent, psychopathology may develop.

These theories served to explain why it is that some people – Evel Knievel and the Great Wallenda, to name only two – were willing, even eager, to risk their lives on a regular basis. Hadn't Maslow told us that the most basic level in the hierarchy of needs was self-preservation? There is, evidently, a more basic need: the preservation of the self-concept! "I am brave, and I am willing to die to preserve that self-image."

Freud and the followers of the psychoanalytical theory, Jung and Adler, principally, were often called the first force in psychology. John B. Watson and B.F. Skinner led the second force. Hayakawa, Rogers, Fritz Perls, Virginia Satir, R.D. Laing and other members the so-called humanistic school were said to be the third force. It is with this group that the Goodfield Method is most closely associated and, in fact, I have worked, in various ways, with each of its members.

Of the current psychotherapies, the Goodfield processes resemble, most closely, Neurolinguistic Programming (NLP), developed by Richard Bandler and John Grinder in the late 60's and early 70's. But, while one may be struck by their similarities, the differences are profound.

Dr. Sieuwko Smith, in his paper on NLP and the Goodfield Method states, "There are some similarities and some fundamental differences between the Goodfield method and Neuro-linguistic Programming (NLP). The similarities are common roots in humanistic psychology and general semantics. The belief that change is possible, the reluctance to label people, the importance of the individual's perception and meta-level symbolization, the special role attributed to non-verbal communication and the necessity of changing a person's "filter of reality," if it does not (or no longer) suit this person's interests. The fundamental differences are that NLP does not work with video, is not interested in traumatic events in the past and considers non-verbal expressions as manifestations of the subconscious and not the unconscious. From this follows that the way the NLP tries to help someone to change his strategy of life is quite different from the way the Goodfield therapist does. One might even ask if NLP is able to touch the "fundamentals of behavior" that have been shaped by important traumatic experiences in the past." (Smith, 1994, The Goodfield Institute)

The method, however, springs from a therapy that contains elements from all the aforementioned disciplines, but it goes beyond them in a number of significant ways. It is the first practical use of the video in therapy; it is the first use of the non-verbal leak as the basis for a complete therapy; it is the only therapy in which the client addresses himself and derives his own interpretation of the manifestations of his unconscious behaviors. Indeed, it is the only therapeutic process to have received a patent from the United States Office of Patents and Copyrights.

2 THE CONSCIOUS AND UNCONSCIOUS SELF-CONCEPTS

The unconscious self-concept is defined as being the individual's awareness of himself in regard to the events of his past, current factors in his life, and the accuracy with which he translates his perception of reality. The more aware the individual becomes, the healthier he will be both mentally and physically.

There are many factors that influence how the individual perceives reality. Among these are his parents and their values, their biases regarding sex role identification, their social and economic position and their religion. How many siblings he has and his position among them play a role. The list goes on.

People who send double messages create unstable relationships that can be profoundly damaging, but they are particularly caustic to the children in whose lives they play key-figure roles. The child learns, for example, that "Later ..." means, "Never ..." and, "yes, but ..." means, "No!" From this and other maladaptive ways of communicating, he internalizes incongruence, unpredictability, and distrust as being normal. But the principal components of a healthy self-concept are predictability, clear boundary setting and unconditional love.

To develop properly, the unconscious self-concept requires regular reinforcement that honestly acknowledges the true aspects of the child's attributes and unique characteristics. The impact of unrealistic expectations placed on the child by his parents or other role models (or himself) can have disastrous repercussions on the developmental process.

To a considerable degree, the parent's perceptions of the child will determine whether he feels accepted; and this leads, in a natural way, to his acceptance of himself. The more he experiences support, the less he will feel stressed and traumatized.

Environmental stability serves to reduce the anxiety that would make the child vulnerable to challenges that would, otherwise, have considerable impact on the development of his unconscious self-concept.

The unconscious self-concept is the collective definitions derived by the individual as a result of unresolved perceived traumatic events. These perceived traumatic events provide a definition regarding the limitations of his capacities, abilities and rights to the expression and gratification of basic human needs.

During the child's development, he may experience events that he perceives as being unbearably shocking or even life threatening whether or not they actually are. We call these occurrences perceived traumatic events, PTEs; and they become the bases for survival strategy decisions. This bundle of strategies solidifies into life-long patterns of behavior that are often inappropriate and/or ineffective, as he grows older, but they remain critical influences in his life.

These old, no longer useful, strategies can manifest themselves in three negative ways: intra-psychically (thought disorders, neuroses), psycho-physiologically (somatic concerns, diseases, illnesses) and interpersonally (relationship difficulties).

When there becomes an increasing difference between the two aspects of the personality (conscious and unconscious), the individual will start to experience more difficulty in dealing with his daily life's decisions due to an increased ambivalence about approaching goals and achieving objectives. A disparity may result from an ever-increasing difference in daily activities versus how the individual feels about himself within himself.

For example, his conscious self-concept may be that he is talented, clever, quick and funny. However, his unconscious self-concept may, at the same time, say just the opposite, that it is only a matter of time until he is discovered as a phony. Did you ever think of a celebrity or public figure whose life ended tragically, and say to yourself, "If I had all that talent, wealth and position, I would surely have done things differently than he did?"

Such names as Mama Cass, of the "Mamas and the Papas," River Phoenix, Judy Garland, John Belushi and the former White House counsel and friend of President Clinton, Vincent Foster, had public personae that were obviously different from their own self images.

It is safe to say that each of these tragic losses reflects an individual story of different circumstances. It is also fair to infer that there was a conclusion that was, to a large degree, motivated by unconscious factors that tipped life's fragile balance fatally.

All were successful, all with great talents, and all had bright futures ahead of them, yet all died tragically.

The explanation can be seen in the obvious incongruence between the unconscious and the self-concept. The unconscious filled with unresolved perceived traumatic events is both powerful and often a source of tragedy.

One of the factors that causes tragedy is a person's inability to receive and accept positive feedback. When we refuse to accept positive input, our reality becomes skewed because positive reinforcement is necessary for proper growth and development.

A person hearing a remark about how good or talented he is may reject this important information in the following way. "This is proof that you do not know me. If you really knew me you would never say what you have just said."

The more an individual is dominated by unconscious feelings reflecting unresolved perceived traumatic events from the past, the more he will find it difficult to accept positive feedback from his surrounding environment in the present.

The pressure to the unconscious self-concept results in part from the fact that the information of a positive nature raises anxiety and increases feelings of alienation. The anxiety increases due to the fact that the information presented is perceived as contrary to, and incongruent with the unconscious experience of himself. The unconscious self-concept provides an image of who the person really is, based upon information not consciously available to awareness but, nonetheless, still having a powerful influence on his actions and image. The famous line of Groucho Marx, says it clearly: "I would not be a member of a club that would have me as a member."

People plagued with this problem find it difficult to be in relationships. Their unconscious self-concept exerts such an influence on their perception that they find it virtually impossible to believe it when their partners say, "I love you."

They say to themselves and sometimes to others, "If you really knew me, you would never say that." They suffer from feelings of alienation and profound feelings of loneliness. They live lives that allow only one type of information to be seen as true and correct, and that information shrivels ultimately to nothingness if they are not treated.

When a person refuses to let in the good news about himself, he is often a poor candidate for therapy. It is the difficult job of the therapist to find the little opening to positive input, and make that opening bigger, and attempt to restore balance. Treatment of individuals in this situation is very difficult. Access to their feelings is limited since they are so overcome by distrust, disbelief and resistance.

A basic principle of psychology is that with stress comes regression. Maybe you have seen someone, in frustration and anger, kicking a flat tire. He had regressed to the behavior of a two-year old, kicking, shouting and looking ridiculous. In most cases this behavior is temporary, but when there are chronic pressures without relief, the system will break down. A certain amount of stress or pressure is natural, normal, and even helpful but, when it is intense and chronic, the unconscious self-concept starts to show signs of collapse. Excessive drinking, fits of anger, drug use and domestic violence, are all chronic signals of danger.

The perceived traumatic events that linger unresolved in the unconscious self-concept, lie in wait for such times when they can pop to the conscious surface, inflicting the fears and frustrations from an unresolved past.

Traumas resulting from other traumas, we call secondary traumas because they can be attributed to one precipitating (primary) trauma. PTEs become compounded as a result of secondary traumas. When traumatic events take place, they have an effect on subsequent events like magnets around slivers of steel. Distrust learned becomes distrust reinforced when similar circumstances recur. The strategy generated during the PTE was an unconscious way of seeking balance and protecting the person from experiencing pain. When a similar situation to the PTE arises again, the old decision – now a new strategy – arises to protect the person.

3 PERCEIVED TRAUMATIC EVENTS

During the formative years of a child's development, a number of events may occur that he perceives as being intensely dangerous or even life threatening. In response to these traumas, the child may unconsciously make decisions regarding how best to deal with these and similar future threats. These decisions become the bases for strategies that he hopes, throughout his life, will serve him successfully when he is confronted with challenges to his safety.

However, the strategy employed at the moment of the perceived traumatic event may have been unrelated to the cessation of the threat. The child unconsciously recognizes simply that he used a process and, from his point of view, it worked; so he uses it again and again with varying degrees of success. It becomes, then, a tool in his repertoire for dealing with conflict in his life, regardless of how inappropriate or ineffective it may be. The event need not be a major one in terms of life or death; the child's translation or perception of what took place will determine whether the event is seen as something that is traumatic.

Some events are truly traumatic, however. An example of a perceived traumatic event (PTE) that came out in a therapy session a few years ago illustrates a reality based PTE.

A client, while in hypnosis, relived a moment that happened when she was three years old. Her mother, hysterical and crying, awakened her as she came into the room where she lay sleeping. The mother had just learned about the death of her husband in an automobile accident. She leaned over her bed crying and screaming, "Your father is dead! Your father is dead! He was just killed in a car accident!"

As a result of that shocking event, my client lost her hearing in the ear that was not covered by the pillow. This is rare but not unheard of in psychology. She understandably did not want to hear this tragic news, so she shut off her hearing in her right ear! She told me later that she never cried about her loss. Apparently she clung to her mother in her shock and tried to console her in her grief. Over the next few years, the hearing loss, which apparently had no organic origin, began to subside and her hearing returned. The perceived traumatic event was so shocking, it put her in a bind with her hysterical mother.

On some level she chose to turn off the source of receiving the unacceptable news, the hearing in her right ear.

When she came out of the hypnosis, she was surprised to still be crying.

She asked, "Why am I still crying? I thought that I would stop. After all, I am no longer in hypnosis."

"Yes," I said, "but your mourning process has just begun."

After the session was over, she told me that she went home and cried for about a month. When her friends would call her on the telephone, she would tell them, when they heard her tears and sadness, that she was crying because her father had died. When they would inquire into the details, she would say, "He died in an automobile accident thirty years ago."

The child's logic and her perception created both the problem and the eventual conclusion. Hypnosis or, more accurately, an altered state of consciousness, is natural and normal but, at the same time, unique. When a person wants to decode some of the issues he may feel inhibit him in contacts with others, both personally and professionally, the clinical use of the Goodfield method is used to explore the origins of the NVL on a deeper clinical level. The objective, however, remains the same: insight and action into areas with limited effective function.

> "Some have argued that hypnosis involves no unusual state of unconsciousness, that it is merely a response to social cues. Most investigators disagree. Although hypnotized individuals are especially sensitive to social cues, their experience as well as their behavior is altered. Perceptions change and movements may seem involuntary and almost automatic. Hypnosis

also produces physiological signs. On EEG examinations, easily hypnotized people have more electrical activity of the type known as theta waves in the left frontal region of the cerebral cortex. Studies measuring the brain's electrical responses to stimuli show specific hypnotic effects on perception. When a person under hypnosis is told to imagine a cardboard box blocking a television screen, the brain's response to the images on the screen is reduced. Hypnosis also reduces the brain's response to a mild shock on the wrist. (This is one basis for its use in pain control.) In two recent studies, measurements of blood flow and metabolic activity by positron emission tomography (PET), have shown that hypnosis activates a part of the brain involved in focusing attention, the anterior cingulate gyrus. There is also evidence that it enhances the activity of dopamine, a neurotransmitter involved in planning, memory, and movement. Thus hypnosis is a neurophysiological reality as well as a psychological and social one."　　　　(Spiegle, 1998)

Perceived traumatic events are perceptions of events that seemed traumatic to an individual, and subsequently affected his strategies. Conflicts within and between individuals are often based on unresolved PTEs. Although an individual involved in crisis management may have little or no clinical interest in the origin of a person's thought formation, the concept of PTEs may be helpful in providing a perspective into often obscure decision-making and position-building.

The altered state is nothing more than an access road into PTEs. Those involved in crisis management and negotiations can infer PTEs by the accurate reading of the NVL of the other person. Just how real are PTEs? To the extent that they profoundly influence the decisions and directions taken by an individual, they may be thought of as the core of his reality.

Controversy has surrounded hypnosis and memory recall. David Spiegle, in the above mentioned article, comments on this:

"The accuracy of hypnotically induced recall is a subject of lively and sometimes angry controversy. Like any method of gaining access to traumatic memories, hypnosis must be used with caution. Although concern about implanting false memories is often exaggerated, it has some basis. Hypnosis is not a truth serum, and the memories it uncovers are no more reliable (but less reliable) than any others. The risk is that hypnotic memories may inspire greater confidence. No memory, whether it is evoked with or without hypnotism, can be shown to be true without corroboration by external evidence. This is a complex and important issue for therapists, because they must be concerned about both suppression of memories and false suggestion."   (Spiegle 1998)

The relationship between memory and judgment is a source of controversy among scholars concerned with this issue. Hastie, R. and Park, B. made the following observation:

"Empirical studies of the relationship between memory and judgment, with subject matter as diverse as social impressions, personal attitudes, attributions of causes for behavior, evaluations of legal culpability, and a variety of probability and frequency estimates, have not revealed simple relations between memory and judgment. Some relationships have been found, but strong empirical relations are rare and results are often contradictory."   (Hastie, 1986)

Some PTEs are simply a matter of memory distortion and a lack of information. For example, a client of mine re-experienced, in an altered state of consciousness, a time when she was lying in her bed as a child. She heard her parents having an argument. She feared that they were going to leave her, and she would be alone and helpless.

She subsequently got in touch with the decision that she took at that time: "I'm never going to argue. I'm going to keep my feelings of anger inside and never let them come out."

Her internist had referred her to me because he was unable to find an organic basis for her complaints. She had stomach problems, migraine headache, and lower bowel difficulties. With the re-evaluation of her old decision, came a reduction of symptoms.

The PTE was communicating its message, which was: "I need to let the fear and pain out, and I will continue to produce these symptoms until I get your attention."

Perceived traumatic events cause problems because, with each PTE, there is an associated decision that accompanies the trauma. These associated decisions are always logical, given the person's perception of the situation. The difficulty arises when a similarly perceived event, against which the adopted strategy is ineffectual, takes place in the future.

4 RESEARCH AND THE NON-VERBAL LEAK AND NON-VERBAL BEHAVIOR

For thirty plus years as the Goodfield Method was being explored and developed with regard to the non-verbal leak in clinical practice, and later with regard to business and governments, others where exploring the subject. The primary consideration of the research was the scientific advancement of basic knowledge about human non-verbal responses to the environment.

There has been a vast body of literature developed in this area. Most have focused upon the conscious aspects of non-verbal behavior and the theoretical research dynamics. When the unconscious aspects were referenced, the repetitive aspects and meaning where rarely if ever mentioned.

A cornerstone of the Goodfield method is the definition of the NVL and its application in clinical and other areas.

Paul Ekman in his book, *Telling Lies: clues to deceit in the marketplace, politics and marriage*, W.W. Norton & Company, New York & London, 1992, gave some interesting findings resulting from his lifelong effort to explore and explain the deeper meanings of the signals sent by people as they attempt to communicate.

Ekman quotes Freud,

> "The suppression of the speaker's intention to say something is the indispensable condition for the occurrence of a slip of the tongue."

The suppression could be deliberate if the speaker were lying, but Freud was more interested in instances in which the speaker is not aware of the suppression. Once the slip occurs, the speaker may recognize what has been suppressed; or, even then, the speaker may not become aware of it.

If the speaker does become aware of his "slip", it may be that he is shocked by hearing his words come out unexpectedly or he may be confronted by his audience's response.

The key to decoding the slip as Freud called it, or the emblematic slip, as Ekman refers to it, or the non-verbal leak, as it is referred to in the Goodfield method, is to notice what transpires just before and just after the observed aspect of the behavior. How do you look at what happened before the observed behavior?

If a person is attempting to mislead someone in a conversation, he may do the following: "I told you that I am not angry; I just think you are wrong."

Let us say that it is the tongue coming out that is first observed. To test for an NVL, two beliefs must be verified.

If it is an NVL, then it will repeat and it will be expressed in the form of a pattern of observable behavior. Two key assumptions are important here.

- Assumption one, if the behavior reflects the unconscious feelings of the person, he will not be aware of what he said.

- Assumption two, if the observable behavior is in fact unconscious, it will repeat itself again and again in the form of a non-verbal pattern.

If the remark is restated as a question, for example, (You say you are not angry. Is that correct?) or in the form of an observation, (You said you are not angry.), the person will, if it is a leak from the unconscious, reproduce the exact same behavioral response to the query again. If the person does not reproduce the same non-verbal behavior to the question or stated observation, then it is not an NVL.

What might be seen if it were an NVL?

"I told you that I am not angry (tongue goes out and in, meaning anger) (eyes close after tongue goes out) I just think you are wrong." (eyes open, lip tightens swallow down.)

The non-verbal leak is the other half of the message. It may be thought of as a more accurate statement of what is truly felt by the person.

What is a possible deeper translation of what is being said in the aforementioned example?

"I told you that I am not angry (tongue goes out and in, message I in fact am angry) eyes close message, I must deny it so I close my eyes to that feeling, (eyes open), top lip tightens message I must control those feelings. Swallow down, message I will swallow those feelings down and say, I just think you are wrong."

Even if a person is trying to deceive someone, it may be reflected in the form of an NVL. When it is a true NVL, it will give guidance to uncovering the deeper message. What are some of the clues to reading what is deliberate lying or deception in a person's message?

Ekman gives a viable definition,

> "I defined lying as a deliberate choice to mislead a target without giving any notification of the intent to do so. There are two major forms of lying: concealment, leaving out true information; and falsification, or presenting false information as if it were true. Other ways to lie include: misdirecting, acknowledging an emotion but misidentifying what caused it; telling the truth falsely, or admitting the truth but with such exaggeration or humor that the target remains uninformed or misled; half concealment, or admitting only part of what is true, so as to deflect the target's interest in what remains concealed; and the incorrect-inference dodge, or telling the truth but in a way that implies the opposite of what is said. There are two kinds of clues to deceit: leakage, when the liar inadvertently reveals the truth; and deception clues, when the liar's behavior reveals only that what he says is untrue."   pp. 41, 42.

How could it be that Freud could have missed the repetitive nature of the "slip" on the non-verbal level? The basic structure of psychoanalysis as practiced by Freud himself gave less emphasis upon non-verbal behavior and more upon the verbal dominations of his patient's interactions. This is not to suggest that Freud did not note an importance of the non-verbal behavior as is quoted earlier in this text.

With regard to Ekman and other researchers, there appears to have been no investigations done into the relationship between the unconscious as observed in non-verbal behavior and patterns of responses.

It is clear in his writings that although not researched thoroughly there is still a belief in what Ekman calls the "embolismic slip" and what in Goodfield is referred to as the non-verbal leak.

Paul Ekman in his book, *Telling Lies* noted that,

> "Unfortunately, none of the other investigators who has studied deceit, have checks to see if they could replicate our finding on emblematic slips. I feel optimistic that they would, having twice over a twenty-five-year period, found leakage through emblematic slips." Also see, Harold G. Johnson, Paul Ekman, and Wallace V. Friesen, "Communicative Body Movements: American Emblems," Semiotica 15, (1975): 335-353.

There have been some peripheral investigations done, however. These are interesting with regard to patterns in the overall system.

> "We endorse the view that emotions involve patterns of responses that have evolved for their ability to organize disparate systems to respond efficiently to critical environmental events. This position – one version of evolutionary emotion theory – postulates different patterns of responses for each emotion, and implies a coherence among behavioral, psychological, and subjective system."
>
> (Darwin, 1872/1965; Ekman, 1977, 1992; Levenson, 1988; Plutchik, 1962; Tomkins, 1962).

Tomkins (1962, pp. 243-244) wrote that affects are sets of organized responses that

> "are capable when activated of simultaneously capturing such widely distributed organs as the face, the heart, and the endocrine, and imposing on them a specific pattern of correlated responses."

In the empirical literature on emotion, evidence is just beginning to appear that there is cohesion among different emotion response domains.

There has been some evidence of coherence between facial expression and self-report of emotion (Ekman,

Friesen & Ancoli, 1980) and for coherence between expression and physiology (Davidson, Ekman, Saron, Senulis & Friesen, 1990).

Ekman goes on to suggest that,

> "Such research, however, has not looked at correspondences among emotional response systems at specific points in time, but rather has evaluated correspondences among response measure from aggregated occurrences of particular emotions across blocks of time. If Tomkins was right, congruence between systems should be evident as on a more momentary basis. During an emotion, changes in expression, physiology, and experience should correspond temporally and categorically. Facial signs of anger should occur with the subjective experience of anger-specific physiological patterns."

Does it not make equal sense that these connections between various systems in the body are linked together? Their effect is to produce congruent messages to a specific emotional situation. When, however, there is a different set of feelings on a conscious and unconscious level, there will be measurable double messages reflecting this incongruence.

This is an example of a leak from the unconscious or, as it is referred to in the Goodfield method, a non-verbal leak.

If, for example, a person tells another that, "I love you", and at the same time looks away and blinks his eyes, this is an incongruent message. It might reflect his unconscious belief, based upon a PTE early in his childhood, that he is incapable of giving love.

He may feel love for another and, at the same time, feel that it is futile to try to act on it. When considering crisis or conflicts in differing countries, it is important to take into consideration the uniqueness of a specific culture i.e., how eye contact differs between cultures. In Japan it is considered a sign of disrespect and, in some cases, even aggressive to look someone directly in the eyes as you express your feelings.

Conversely, in America and other western countries, we make negative judgments when someone refuses to make eye contact when speaking to a person. This does not suggest that there is not a positive relationship between what we feel, either consciously or unconsciously, and what we show non-verbally. Emotions are universal; and responses seem to reflect this fact.

Cross-cultural aspects of non-verbal responses suggest that the NVL should not be thought of as culture bound to one group or another.

In a book titled, Body Language, by Julius Fast, the author describes a study done by Ekman, Sorenson and Friesen. They had conducted studies in New Guinea, Borneo, the United States, Brazil and Japan, five widely different continents, and discovered:

> "Observers in these cultures recognize some of the same emotions when they are shown a standard set of facial photographs." According to the three men, this contradicts a theory that facial displays of emotion are socially learned. They also feel that there is agreement within a culture on recognizing different emotional states."
>
> Ekman, Sorenson and Friesen, 1969.

To those potentially involved in conflict resolution and crisis management, the research conducted by Paul Ekman is of interest in that it offers some guidance in "reading" the credibility of those who might practice deception or outright lying in conflict situations.

He offers these findings:

> "The lie catcher must be cautious, not assuming that any slip of the tongue is evidence of lying. Usually the context in which a slip occurs should help in figuring out whether or not the slip is betraying a lie. The lie catcher must also avoid the error of considering someone truthful just because there are no slips of the tongue. Many lies do not contain any."

Freud did not explain why some lies are betrayed by slips while most are not. It is tempting to think that slips occur when the liar wants to be caught, when there is guilt about lying to his esteemed colleague.

But there has been no study, or even much speculating, that would explain why only certain lies are betrayed by slips.

There is a possible area of disagreement between positions held in the Goodfield method and some of the positions held by Ekman.

> "Some people always talk in a circumlocutious fashion, but few people make emblematic slips regularly. Speech errors may signify stress of many kinds, not necessarily just the stresses involved in lying."

The frequency of NVL's is a regular occurrence with people, in that the unconscious is always seeking expression on the conscious level, hence the slip that Freud noted. The degree to which a person is repressed will be an important factor in the frequency of his NVL's.

Perhaps an explanation for the why only certain lies are betrayed by slips is that, when there is a slip or an NVL, it is reflecting the other half of the person's message, and it is not a "lie" as such; it is just not a full statement of what the individual really feels. Moreover, it reflects the ambivalence that exists between the two levels of consciousness. A lie on the other hand, is as Ekman says," a deliberate choice to mislead a target without giving any notification of the intent to do so."

It is a given fact in psychology that with stress goes regression. Pressure pushes people to return to earlier patterns of behavior. When this happens, there is a greater chance of an individual exhibiting a leak from the unconscious.

Old unresolved fears and traumas are more likely to surface at these times and therefore, there is a higher probability of an NVL occurring.

Crisis situations are sure to surface a number of strategies within people as they attempt to drop pressure and overcome obstacles. Ekman discusses another aspect of deception that may surface in these situations.

"Tirades are a third way (there are four sources of leakage, slips of the tongue, tirades, emblematic slips and micro expressions) liars may betray themselves in words. A tirade is different from a slip of the tongue. The speech blunder is more than a word or two. The information doesn't slip out; it pours out.

The liar is carried away by emotion, not realizing until afterward the consequences of what he is revealing. Often, if the liar had remained cool, he would not have revealed the damaging information. It is the pressure of overwhelming emotion – fury, horror, terror, or distress – that causes the liar to give away information."

What is critical to keep in mind is that each person is unique in his past experiences. Those past experiences, good or bad, resolved or still traumatic, are important factors in what he brings to a conflict. Although there is much known about the non-verbal behavior of people certain things must be remembered. Ekman reminds us,

"What for most people might be a clue to deceit is not for such a person.

Some people:

- are indirect and circumlocutious in their speech;
- speak with many short or long pauses between words;
- make many speech errors;
- use few illustrations;
- make many body manipulations;
- often show signs of fear, distress, or anger in their facial expressions regardless of how they actually feel;
- show asymmetrical facial expressions."

Paul Ekman, Telling Lies, Page 166.

A person assessing an individual in a crisis situation should establish a baseline of behavioral responses of the person that he is going to "read".

We are the "presents" of the past and each past is different as are the NVL's associated with that past.

Of this Ekman says,

> "The only way to reduce mistakes due to the Brokaw hazard (the possibility of misjudging someone) is to base judgment on a change in the suspect's behavior. The lie catcher must make a comparison between the suspect's usual behavior and the behavior shown when the suspect is under suspicion. People are likely to be misled in first meetings because there is no base of comparison, no opportunity to note changes in behavior. Absolute judgments – she is doing so many manipulator actions that she must be very uncomfortable about something she is not saying – are likely to be wrong."
>
> Ekman P.

Careful and systematic use of the procedures to determine a non-verbal leak can be helpful in dealing more effectively with a crisis. When a person fails to learn completely or fails to follow the protocol, he may exacerbate a situation with misinformation and faulty interpretations.

The skill necessary to "read" others can be learned if the student learns the basic data about non-verbal behavior and the NVL. The Goodfield Institute has, for more than thirty years, offered instruction in this skill.

What is interesting is that one might think that psychologists, psychiatrists, people in law enforcement, FBI, CIA and those involved in executive protection would do better than the general population individual in "reading" the attempts at deception and lying. This is not the way it turned out when a study was conducted that considered this question.

> "In September 1991, our findings on these professional lie catchers were published. It turned out that only one occupational group did better than chance – the U.S. Secret Service. A little more than half of them scored at or above 70 percent level accuracy, nearly a third reached 80 percent or more.

Although I cannot be certain why the Secret Service did so much better than the other groups, my bet is that it is because many of them had done protection work – watching crowds for any sign of someone who might menace the person they were protecting. That kind of vigilance should be very good preparation for spotting the subtle behavioral clues to deceit."

Ekman P.

It is possible to spot deception or a non-verbal leak if there is a pressure in the situation such as a crisis or a conflict. Here the lack of time in contact with the person that is to be "read" may be compensated for by an increased intensity of his response.

Ekman came to a similar conclusion.

"The lie catcher does not need to know as much about either the suspect or the situation if strong emotions are aroused."

Ekman, P.

What are the signs that may be helpful to learn to know if you are being deceived?

There are some guidelines:

The literature on psychophysiological markers of lying (e.g. Lykken, 1979) shows that deception is usually associated with increases in arousal. Non-verbal indicators of arousal, such as blinking, pupil dilation, pitch, speech errors, and speech hesitations might therefore occur in increased frequency when a sender is lying. A third source of deceptive markers are indicators of affective states such as guilt or shame (Kraut, 1980) or "duping delight" (the reaction of another that gives joy to the lie teller) (Ekman, 1980). Generally, neither guilt and shame nor "duping delight" are likely to occur in the laboratory to a marked degree, but one might think that most subjects do not like to deceive, and might therefore show some signs of anxiety such as less eye contact, less direct body orientation and more distance from the communication partner (Mehrabian, 1971), as well as a decrease in the use of illustrators (Ekman, 1980). Lastly, it is generally assumed that producing a deceptive message is cognitively more demanding than telling a simple truth. Senders of deceptive messages should therefore show indicators of cognitive effort such as speech pauses, longer response latencies, pupil dilation, and fewer illustrators (Goldman-Eisler, 1968; Kahneman, 1973; Ekman & Friesen, 1972).

It is important for those involved in crisis management to remember a few things. You are probably going to have a more lasting success in resolving conflict if you work toward a win-win outcome. This effort in itself will, by definition, reduce deception, deceit and lying. If both sides of a conflict approach each other with this attitude, conflict will beget communication, and that will increase the chance that it will be a lasting one.

Unfortunately not all participants in a crisis hold such an enlightened viewpoint. Learning the techniques of determining deception will produce a greater sense of confidence within those dealing with difficulties.

It is important to remember the findings regarding professional's skills in "reading" others. Few did better than chance.

This need not be of great concern to those charged with dealing with conflict if their approach is clear and their eyes are open. The other side in a conflict wants victory too. It is the job of those involved, in resolving it to define victory in a bipartisan way, when possible.

The research into non-verbal behavior sheds light on the way we attempt to influence each other on a conscious level. It sheds light on our actions on a deep psychophysiological level. It gives a perspective of the complexity of human interactions. Moreover, it can help to make us more aware of ourselves as communicators.

Before any serious crisis management or conflict resolution is to take place it would do well for those involved in resolving the difficulty to read, analyze and be clear about the conscious and unconscious messages of those involved. Research has shown:

> "Facial expressions are a remarkable indicator of emotion. Facial expressions correlate with the self-reported experience of emotion (Ekman, Friesen &

Ancoli, 1980; Keltner, 1995) as well as with patterns of autonomic nervous system (Levenson, Ekman, Saron, Senulius & Friesen, 1990). The study of facial expression offers researchers a window into complex emotional processes as they unfold dynamically."

It is in most cases impossible to pick the players in a crisis or conflict with whom we must negotiate.

Stress and pressure to win or find a successful outcome in a conflict can result in those involved showing psychological behaviors that are usually shown only at home or office.

5 THE NON-VERBAL LEAK

The non-verbal leak (NVL) is an often extraordinarily rapid, repetitive, patterned series of movements recorded from the shoulders up, reflecting an unresolved perceived trauma and manifesting a decision and a strategy from the past, a decision and strategy believed to have been appropriate at the time, but that is maladaptive here and now. The trauma – any event that is life threatening or perceived to be life threatening – creates a state of imbalance within the individual, and reflects retention, a holding in of the tension.

The NVL is the silent language of the unconscious, another part of our communications repertoire; and it can be read just as any other language can be read. In fact, many people, without any training at all, seem to have a natural talent for reading NVLs. Others have learned the so-called body language principles. They believe that a person who crosses his arms while he talks is hiding something; a leg moving up and down indicates aggression. Well, yes and no. *Hasta la vista* has one meaning when friends wave goodbye at the airport, but an entirely different one when Arnold Schwarzenegger blows up the airport! Just as your own language has patterns unique to you, so it is with regard to your non-verbal language. Context determines meaning; perception determines reality.

When the NVL is read correctly, however, it can unlock many mysteries. Why are some relationships doomed from the start? Why are some of us our own worst enemies? Why do we make ourselves sick or insane?

Still, being able to more accurately read these messages from the unconscious does not mean that one will magically find success and happiness. It is not a parlor game skill to use on people. It is simply another life-viewing tool, albeit an extraordinarily powerful one that provides a deeper understanding of one's self and those around him. That knowledge tends to change life for the better because, when we can literally see and understand the messages from the unconscious, we can truly become the masters of our own destinies.

Why do we have non-verbal leaks and where do they come from? The answer is that the human being needs and strives for balance. When he communicates about a subject that has meaning for him or consequences regarding his response, there is a pressure in his system to express the whole truth.

By expressing his total feeling, especially when he is ambivalent about an issue, he retains or restores balance within himself. A double message or incongruent message is, in fact, an example of the system trying to express a more complete or congruent message of what he really feels. An old experience in his life has served as a learning point on a conscious level or a perceived traumatic event (PTE) when on an unconscious level. When an event in the here and now triggers an old decision from the past, that old decision will be reflected in the here and now in the form of a non-verbal leak if the unconscious message is not congruent with the old decision.

When we perceive incongruence in an individual, it stands out as something that influences our memory. Somehow, the behavior we see does not to fit into our recollection of our experience with this person. The non-verbal leak is, by definition, a double message; and often we remember or are struck by the inconsistency between what an individual says and how he reflects that on a non-verbal level. As we look at the incongruence, it can create an imbalance within ourselves because somehow the behavior does not fit.

Hastie and Kumar (1979, replicated by many others, most notably Srull, 1981) found that when subjects studied sentences describing the behavior of a hypothetical character while making judgments of the character's personality, behaviors that were incongruent with the final trait ratings were the best recalled on a subsequent memory test. This reversal of the commonly expected direct memory-judgement relationship has been explained as resulting from "special processing" accorded to the incongruent acts when they were attributed to a single character in the context of an impression formation task (Hastie, 1984). Empirical results suggest that this special processing involves the subject's effort to explain why the surprising, incongruent actions were performed by the character, a plausible subtask within the larger impression formation task. The non-verbal leak is the other half of our message.

For example, if your old experiences taught you on an unconscious level (PTE) that it is not safe to show what you feel and you, on a conscious level, find yourself feeling love for someone, an inconsistency exists within your system. The system, in an effort to reduce the inconsistency, sends both messages, one on conscious level and another on an unconscious level. The messages are presented as incongruences between verbal and non-verbal levels, the non-verbal reflecting the unconscious aspect of what we feel. This is the origin of the non-verbal leak, which originates from a perceived traumatic event. The non-verbal leak can be broken down to three basic components: first, what I initially felt, secondly, what I initially wanted to do, and, finally, what I actually did.

The actual non-verbal responses are decoded into their unconscious symbolic meaning or A, R1 and R2. We may consider again the previous example. You verbally say, "I love you." Your non-verbal leak, as you say those words, shows, I (eyes open) love (eyes closed) you (eyes closed, top lip tightened, and swallowing down). The complete message, then, is: I love you, however, I am anxious about telling you that because in the past I had bad experiences giving my love to others. I have subsequently learned to avoid these areas, and I close-up when they arise in my life.

This message, while a true and complete one, is not necessarily the best opening line in a new relationship. Both messages come out, one heard and the other felt on some level. There may be various explanations for this behavior but, once again, the key issue is to see and hear the communication from both levels of consciousness. Here lies the basis for successful communication. In crisis situations, the pressure is higher than in normal circumstances. One can expect the NVL to be more apparent, as both halves of the message seek expression. As adversaries seek compromises or total victory, other NVLs will become more apparent and therefore, better tools to probe deeper into the real agenda.

In order to gain the benefits of this important information, the reader of the NVL must perform one more step. The next step is to raise from the non-verbal level to the symbolic level the hard data that has been gathered. Here the raw data is interpreted into clear and usable symbolic meaning. When the task at hand is a therapeutic one, a clinical plan for treatment will emerge from the data.

The raw data is the observed repetitive responses noted as the person speaks. The interpretation begins when that information becomes the basis for what is referred to as the symbolic level. When the NVL is being used as a means of gathering deeper underlying motivations of an action, a tactical plan of attack will emerge. The hard data of the NVL can be used tactically or clinically depending on the need and/or objective. The person having the NVL data should consider the moral judgements and their impact on the emotions. Lennart Sjoberg, Center for Risk Research, Stockholm School of Economics, Sweden, makes the following observation:

> "Although it can be debated whether moral judgment is entirely cognitive, it is certainly closely related to emotional processes. Indignation involves anger, and hence emotional reactions should not be neglected in any discussion of risk perception. They may even be of major importance and a more important source of the societal problems connected with varying risk perception than cognitive biases." (Sjoberg)

It is at this point that issues of ethics and morality must be considered. Short term victory, when based upon trickery or treachery, usually results in an inequality, disharmony and ultimate instability. Look at any area in the world where there is injustice felt by one faction about another, and you will see the bases for crisis. The NVL is used most effectively to search out deeper levels of difference with the goal of resolving them as opposed to exploiting them. When the non-verbal leak is taken to the symbolic level for further analysis, the concept of Action, Reaction and Reaction to the Reaction is used. The non-verbal leak is the referential level of behavior. The A, R1, R2, is the symbolic level.

6 THE SYMBOLIC LEVEL OF THE NON-VERBAL LEAK, A, R1, R2

If conflict is to be overcome, and crisis is to be avoided, understanding is critical. Observations of referential data need to be translated into useable information. That is what the symbolic level of the NVL is. When we decode the total conscious and unconscious messages of the person, real crisis management can take place with the greater possibility of lasting, successful results. The action (A) is rooted in any perceived traumatic event (PTE). It is real in the eyes of the person who experienced it. This shock to the system can be recorded on both levels of consciousness. Moreover, it impacts upon the person on an intrapsychic, psycho-physiological or interpersonal level.

The reaction (R1) to the action is the first impulse that the person has to the traumatic event. It is what he really wants to do. If his response to the situation is anger in the R1 stage, he wants to express it clearly and directly with no holding back. The reaction to the reaction (R2) is what the person really does. It is not what he wants to do. He may feel rage but he realizes that, if he gives in to these feelings, he could make the situation even worse. This is where the person finds a compromise that works for him at that moment. In psychoanalytic theory the concept of the id, ego and superego seek to explain the decision making process. Freud's idea's are hypothetical constructs, that add understanding to the decision making process. Action, reaction and reaction to the reaction also help to decode the decision making process, however the A. R1 and R2 are observable, testable realities.

With time and similar perceptions of what his world is like, he develops repetitive strategies for similar situations. It could be said that the R2 is the person's basic strategy in dealing with those feelings in his life.

The NVL is reflected not just in the upper part of the person; it is shown throughout the person's body in his movements. This more complete expression of the unconscious messages of the person is referred to as the BNVL or the body non-verbal leak.

7 THE BODY NON-VERBAL LEAK

We are a psychophysiological system and, therefore, we must consider the total body. I refer to this aspect as the Body Non-Verbal Leak (BNVL). In crisis management and conflict resolution, as you attempt to resolve the conflict, it is critical to observe the key people as they express their feelings. The observation of specific behavior, such as arm and leg movements and breathing patterns reflect some of the body movements which must be considered. Reading the total system's reactions is what is meant when we decode the body non-verbal leak. The observed behavior, when seen in repetitive pattern form, provides the basis for the subsequent interpretation observation.

As a result of close observation and analysis, we can see the physical responses of the system throughout the total body. The BNVL reflects the total recorded factors of a perceived trauma within the system. This observable unconscious movement forms the basis for the clinical intervention into the patient's system.

Trauma is a state of imbalance within the individual, and reflects retention, which is a matter of holding tension inside. Our attempts to achieve balance often generate more imbalances. Think of a time when you lost your balance and stumbled on a staircase. Often our attempt to regain balance results in more imbalance, and we may trip even more and fall. Balance and imbalance are daily factors in our lives, and are reflected in our bodies actions and functions. If we are to move forward in our efforts, there are basic ideas to keep in mind, as they will have impact on the degree of success or failure in dealing with conflicts. There are three key concepts in life: insight, action and risk taking. By risk taking, an individual places himself in a position where something might go wrong; however something might go very right, also. Risk taking is a matter of self-concept in a certain way. How you see yourself will affect what you do with regard to the opportunities with which you are presented on a daily basis. An interesting study considered entrepreneurs and their behavior:

"Although spectators may judge that entrepreneurs take more risks than the average person, entrepreneurs see themselves as not being particularly risk prone."
(Keyes, 1985, pp. 207-209; McClelland, 1961, p. 222).

This is also true of people who engage in physically risky professions or hobbies:

"First they challenge fate, and then they try to bullwhip fate to its knees by making their adventure as predictable as possible. In fact, it's not adventure they're after. It's mastery."   (Keyes, 1985, p.115).

"Even in casino gambling, where outcomes cannot be controlled, high-stakes gamblers take pride in the control of their emotions."   (See, for example, Alvarez, 1983, pp. 47, 169; Thackrey, 1968, pp. 62-63).

In a clinical setting, the adventure in which the therapist and client find themselves, insight has led to an understanding. A discovery, within the controlled risk of therapy, has taken place. What is meant by discovery is finding something that was already there. No person can discover something unless it was already there. The team sets out to discover the hidden messages heretofore locked in the recesses of the unconscious. They have found the map revealing the special movements that must be observed, traced, tracked and followed. They have achieved a level of insight, which metaphorically places them in front of a large door, behind which lie the secrets to the puzzle that begins the adventure. The door has been locked, and access forbidden for years.

If the adventure is to continue, a key must be found to open the door. The territory can be explored and the secrets brought to the level of consciousness only after access has been obtained. Myths and mysteries exist as speculation without insight and substantive action. That action requires risk-taking on the part of team members.

What could go wrong now? Inherent to the idea of risk taking is the notion of failure. Access could fail, leaving the client with insight only; but insight without action leads to anxiety. It was some level of anxiety or feeling of unrest that started the process, so there is really nothing to lose by continuing the effort if it does not succeed at first.

When an individual is involved in the clinical/therapeutic aspects of the Goodfield method, communication still remains a prime motivating force in the actions of those involved. When the BNVL, which reflects the unconscious movements of the person, is being explored, access to the unconscious behavior, heretofore blocked to conscious awareness, must be obtained. In order to deal precisely with the BNVL (the territory) the person will need to go into hypnosis or, more accurately, an altered state of consciousness. The old general semantics idea promoted by S.I. Hayakawa, Pemberton and others is a useful concept idea here. It basically makes reference to the difference between the symbol and what it symbolizes. The non-verbal leak is a symbolic representation of a R2 strategy that is most clearly seen and treated in its bodily manifestation, namely the BNVL. The key to unlocking the perceived traumatic events, which form the unconscious self-concept is hypnosis. Here a qualified therapist is needed. With the person in a mild hypnosis, the client's bodily reactions are watched carefully for indications of the contractions and movements that reflect the unconscious process. The body becomes a kind of road with subtle turns and changes in direction. The human strives for balance. The movements are logical and often very subtle. Here is where the therapist's years of training in observational skills pay off. The key to the unconscious secrets may not lie in what the client does, but in what he does *not* do. When a person blocks his breathing or somehow restricts his normal movements, this can reveal important information. It may reveal anxiety in relation to an immediate event or anxiety as he recalls a previous event. What is important is that, by noting the change in behavior, one potentially gleans a deeper view into the person's thought processes.

Perhaps one of the most difficult concepts for a person to learn is the idea of no behavior, what it means to a therapist when he sees nothing; but no behavior is behavior. If you don't do something, that's something. My belief in this concept was profoundly tested along with the idea of the BNVL and hypnosis one afternoon in Paris.

My client was a top leader in the resistance against the French during the French Algerian war. We were meeting in London to explore some personal issues he had. He was an aristocratic military figure with great control and superior intelligence and an air of quiet dignity. We had been meeting for five days, primarily in what was a series of intellectual discussions about the feasibility of change within a person. It was a kind of therapeutic foreplay.

Much of our discussion focused on World War II generals who symbolically represented different styles of leadership and approaches to risk taking. Fortunately, I was fairly well informed on the subject, but I was becoming frustrated and impatient because I wanted to get on with the work.

On the last day he had to make the decision as to whether he was willing to try to explore his problems in hypnosis. At lunch he announced his decision.

"Yes, it's two o'clock now, and I will need to stop at five so I can catch my flight home."

By the time we got started, it was close to 3 p.m. That left about two hours to do the work.

The pressure was on and I wondered if this was not some kind of unconscious manipulation on his part to avoid dealing with the problem that we had been skirting for many days.

I began the process of hypnotic induction. He lay there not moving as I continued counting slowly, 3-2- and 1, 3-2- and 1. Nothing was happening, nothing at all. There was no movement, and even worse, he began to snore! I continued counting and, as I did, I raised my voice. Still nothing happened. I remembered a remark I often had made to others: No problem can be resolved on the level at which it develops. You must somehow get above the problem and see it from another perspective.

I asked myself, "What is really going on here? Nothing, absolutely nothing. There is no behavior. That's right, no behavior, but no behavior is behavior." I looked even closer now, and noticed there was an almost imperceptible movement coming from a muscle in his left thigh. No behavior is, ultimately, masked behavior. Over the snoring, which had grown even louder, I instructed him to make the feelings in his left leg even stronger. I carefully put one finger on the pulsing muscle.

"Be at the time and place that relates to this movement."

Suddenly his back arched and he moaned. The BNVL started to show more now. Both legs moved as if he were trying to walk. After a few minutes, his body stopped moving. I asked him if he was aware of any decision that he had taken at that time and place.

"Yes," he whispered.

"Review that situation and see if you can find a new and more appropriate decision that is correct for your life now."

He indicated that he had. I counted him out of the hypnosis.

"What was the situation, and the old and new decision?"

He sat up and explained what had happened.

"Because we were a small fighting force and needed to move to different locations, we fought during the day and traveled at night. We marched in pairs in a special way, one man staying awake and guiding the other while he slept.

"One night, as I was sleep-marching, I was shot by a sniper or perhaps by one of my own men. The result was a long-term hospitalization and a short unconscious decision never to trust anybody again. My new decision is to give people a chance. After all, not every person is a sniper or an angry soldier."

Within a few minutes, we shook hands politely and he left to catch his plane. That team adventure had a good conclusion, thanks in part to the BNVL and trust in the process. It taught me, again, that nothing could really be something, sometimes.

Each time we deal with the BNVL, we are working with three different levels of the system: action, reaction and the reaction to the reaction (A, R1 and R2). With A, R1 and R2 we can look at how a perceived trauma is recorded within the system and how someone reacts to that perceived trauma. The non-verbal leak is the referential level of behavior. The A, R1, R2 is the symbolic level. To sum up the basic methods which are used to resolve conflict and reduce crisis, whether analyzing or treating, we do the following: First there is the video from which the NVL is deduced. Next the symbolic decoding of the NVL takes place. This is where the basic strategies are formulated and a practical plan is made to resolve the presenting conflict.

8 THE INTERACTIVE NON-VERBAL LEAK

Sometimes, when I meet a couple and watch the way they relate to each other, I am in a quandary as to who will kill whom first, but much of the inexplicable behavior can be clarified by considering the real reasons they are together. The concept of the interactive non-verbal leak (INVL) can perhaps shed some light on seemingly bizarre ways that some couples interact. The INVL, which is from the past, can be defined as an accumulative, non-verbal response in terms of three factors: A, R1 and R2, where A is the initial action, R1 is the reaction to the action, and R2 is the reaction to that reaction. It is the sum total of an individual's interaction regarding the expression of basic emotional strategies. These strategies are internalized by an individual in relation to another individual's strategies regarding his or her expression of basic feelings. They result in NVLs, which incorporate the basic aspects of the couple's interactions on both conscious and unconscious levels.

For example, one individual's NVL may express the unconscious statement: "I can't stand aggression." Another individual's NVL may express: "I can't give aggression." When they meet, they have the feeling they were made for each other, but this feeling may be based on their compatible pathologies. They are simply having a job-interview style of conversation but, basically, the non-verbal is the central communication point.

The bonding between these two may reflect a reluctance to be become involved in aggressive behavior.

There is, however, deeper, unconscious meaning, perhaps. Unresolved past traumatic events may have pre-programmed them to avoid individuals with styles of expressing aggression that reflect their past traumatic experiences.

From this unconscious tennis match comes an unconscious contract. The couple feels so comfortable with each other that, over time, they decide to marry but, under the pressures of daily life, there will be uproar in their marriage. In the therapist's office, one of them will say something like, "Something is wrong. You have changed, and I don't like it."

You can be sure, in this case, that one of them has broken the contract either by growing or by not growing at the rate or pace of the other. When this betrayal occurs, it is associated with considerable anxiety and pain, which can be alleviated only by re-evaluation, modification, adaptation, separation, or divorce.

Many years ago I had a woman in therapy and, after a few meetings, I invited her husband to a session so their relationship could be explored. He was a giant compared to her. She was so small that her feet barely touched the floor; he stuffed himself into the largest chair in the room.

For the next hour, I listened to her tell him what an overbearing tyrant he was, how he intimidated her with his size and power, charges to which he admitted his guilt. It quickly became clear that this was their unique form of relating to one another. He was defensive about his size and fearful of overwhelming her, and she was angry about being so small that she was determined to fight this injustice.

It finally came out that he had had a mother who was overwhelming, and he was struggling to be himself while, at the same time, trying not to overwhelm his wife.

She, on the other hand, had a father and three brothers who badgered her about her small size.

Their marriage was a constant struggle for power to achieve balance. Her non-verbal behaviors were consistent with her emotions: her eyes flared, her tongue darted out and then she would swallow down, signaling, "I am furious, and I will make you pay for your actions. You are ganging up on me just like my dad and brothers did."

He reacted by rolling his eyes up, clenching his jaws and then swallowing down, non-verbally stating: "I don't want to be here. It's the same old stuff, and it makes me angry. I will escape by trancing out."

Not all couples who join together in the attempt to resolve their PTEs in their relationships that begin with INVLs, are doomed to pain and suffering, but the INVL is a fact that influences how couples relate to each other. There are other factors, of course. Our parents and their parents and even earlier generations play their roles in our decisions, our actions, our views, and our values. We call this phenomenon the historical interactive non-verbal leak (HINVL).

9 THE HISTORICAL INTERACTIVE NON-VERBAL LEAK – THE GIFT THAT KEEPS ON GIVING

When a stone hits a pond, a series of concentric circles radiate outward. The radiation reflects the intensity of the stone's impact. So it is with perceived traumatic events (PTEs).

Imagine a few small boats positioned at various points along the epicenter of a pond, one of the boats exactly positioned at the initial point of impact, another at the first concentric circle, and still another at the second, etc. etc. Of course, at the fifth or sixth concentric circle, the small boat will experience less distortion and impact than the boat at the center.

If there were people on these imaginary boats, there would be sketchier primary information about the causality, origin, and implication as a result of their differing distances from ground zero. The consequence would be an increased speculation on the part of those at greater distances. So it is with the historical interactive non-verbal leak. As the HINVL's definition suggests, past PTE's impact upon individuals in a family from one generation to the next.

When an individual has a major PTE, that is not resolved in some satisfactory way, it will be passed along to the children in the family and their children and theirs until resolution is found. The primary mode of transmission is through non-verbal messages that reflect the old strategies that resulted from the old decisions in relationship to the event that was initially perceived as a traumatic event. All of this is communicated, not only on a non-verbal level; it is transmitted on an unconscious level as well. Actions, when reflecting an HINVL, are often taken, but are usually not questioned. When they are questioned, the remarks made are usually vague and reflecting more of a feeling tone that says, :"I do not know why I do this or feel this way. We (fill in a family name) have done this in this way for generations. We have been always stoic and held our deeper feelings inside."

These remarks reflect values and tradition. When they don't result in repetitive pathological responses to the environment, these actions usually go on unchallenged by the unconscious mind.

When, however, the person is daily impacted by a vague feeling of uneasiness or discomfort, the HINVL may be pushing an unresolved issue from someone else's past. In that sense, we are the "presents" of the past, the boat at the epicenter. Ultimately, the person here and now has an NVL that shows his unconscious signal of an emotional need. We need contact and affection but, if we have been taught that we of this family are unable to be successful at achieving real contact and intimacy, then we either don't try or, when we do, we somehow unconsciously sabotage our efforts. The HINVL is an unconscious self-fulfilling prophecy that shapes our lives and influences the directions we take. When we consider this in terms of crisis management, the implications are both clear and profound. To illustrate the role of the HINVL, I usually tell the following story so a person may see how an event, generations past, can influence our lives today. This is a fictitious tale, but the HINVL influencing you today is not.

It is prudent for those involved in crisis management to be aware of the unquestioned biases passed down to them. It is a gift that keeps on giving until it is refused.

In 1805, we have the captain of a big sailing ship who fights in the battle of Trafalgar. He defines himself as a strong, courageous risk taker, who has a charming, faithful wife waiting for him to come home.

In an encounter with the French fleet, he is struck by a cannon ball and he loses his leg.

When he comes home, he and his wife agree that his tragedy was caused by his reckless, risk-taking life style. When their son is born, he is given the message, almost from birth through his childhood and beyond, that risk taking is dangerous and is to be avoided. Later, he meets and marries a woman whose search is for security, and he is everything she hoped for: solid, reliable, responsible and predictable. He is, in fact, behaving as if the event on the ship had happened to him.

The years go by and, several generations later, a conservative fellow obsessed with the proper ways to behave, is living an anorexic, sterile, but sensible life based on what he calls "our family values." He has gone to the right schools, done the right things, always played it safe. His world gets smaller and smaller as he is more and more offended by people whom he considers foolish, behaving outrageously in public.

He and his wife eventually come into therapy because their marriage has gone flat, and they don't know why, and they don't believe in divorce. When the therapist suggests trying different approaches, they resist on the grounds that they've always done it this way.

"Does it work?" the therapist asks. "I notice that, when you talk about your great-great-great grandfather, your eyes light up. Why is that?"

"He was a great naval officer. He was a hero."

"There is a part of you that is very attracted to him and what he did and his style of life, but there is another part of you that says there is also something dangerous about that. Is there a bit of him in you?"

When the young man looks objectively at his life, he sees that there are changes he can make. He doesn't have to lose his leg in battle; he can change his life by simply expanding his schema. He always wanted to have a red sports car, and ride with the top down. His secret wish was to make love to his wife with the lights on. He realizes that these and other fantasies, when brought to fruition, would enhance his life. The thrill he felt when he visualized himself announcing his new persona encouraged him to act on it as soon as possible.

So, what we find here, is that all these generations had the thought of risk-taking; but what is important is the relationship between insight, understanding and action. Insight without action creates anxiety. Action without insight creates chaos. Action with insight allows for successful risk taking in the here and now, aware of the needs and demands of the environment, allowing one to confront those needs with his own abilities and desires to forge his world his way.

One need only look at a map and find Bosnia, Serbia, Israel, Palestine, North Ireland, Iran, Iraq, Pakistan, India and the other war-torn societies. Many of the conflicts are still being fought, and the origins or PTEs are obscured with time, and misperceived or distorted.

What hope is there for those people locked in historical conflicts not of their immediate making? If there is hope, it rests in the awareness that violence begets violence, and that violence reflects a communication about a lack of communication.

The person charged with resolving or bringing about peace or holding hostilities in check, must deal with the person in front of him and that person's idea of the origins and implications of the conflict. He must be clear about his role and power to affect the perceived crisis, and he must keep in mind that his true feelings may not reflect his government's or company's policy in the matter. He must also be aware of his non-verbal messages and those of his negotiation team if he is to communicate and not escalate the situation.

Basic skill in reading NVLs is a most useful tool in surfacing hidden agendas and unaware assumptions. The ability to accurately read the total message of the system is, of course, equally critical and, therefore, the HINVL factors will also be of great importance. The past is presented in our present strategies. Sometimes, we must understand the messages of the past in order to avoid reproducing them in the present.

Bias, bigotry and belligerence from past times can and do affect negotiations in the present. The Arab-Israeli conflicts have developed generations of polarized people. This is true in so many crises that affect our lives today.

How do you know when you are looking at a deep-seated set of biases from the person's history? The key factor is continuing references to issues not in consideration at the moment. When something mentioned, or clearly implied, reflects a hidden agenda, there may be a closed-minded response to historical factors surrounding the issue at hand. When this seems to dominate a negotiation, there is likely an HINVL issue working.

If balance or resolution to any conflict is to last, it must be based on understanding and mutual respect of those involved in the conflict. If a settlement is not based upon these assumptions, there is a great chance that the agreement, treaty or peace plan will unravel and, even worse, setbacks will result in the risk taking, resulting in failure once again.

10 CONFLICT RESOLUTION AND HINVL CONSIDERATIONS

A negotiator, when entering the room, must remember a number of factors to achieve a successful outcome in his contacts. Sometimes an issue is presented as being non-negotiable. I have spent most of my professional life negotiating the non-negotiable. I am convinced that it is, in most cases, possible to achieve agreement. Sometimes the past is an obstacle to a settlement to conflict and crisis. There are some things to consider as the negotiations begin.

The person sitting at the other side of the table has more than likely been chosen for his skill, reputation, position, approach and communication style. He therefore is not only your adversary, but is also a representative from the other side in the conflict as to how much they value this particular negotiation, and what they want to communicate initially. Know their view of the origins and implications of the conflict. Perhaps the technique of listening and reflecting, often associated with Dr. Carl Rogers, is most helpful here. Listening and reflecting may seem an easy and clear concept, however it is not as easy as it might seem on first consideration. It begins with a genuine desire to understand the other's position. The next challenge is to attempt to restate it to his satisfaction.

"Let me see if I understand you clearly, you are saying XYZ and are not saying ABC. Is that correct?" When the other person sees that you are really trying to understand, a few important things happen. The tendency to overstate the other sentences will be reduced. Massive generalizations will decrease. The anger hostility tends to be replaced with concentration in an attempt to understand. Most importantly, the feeling tone changes to one of good will and tends toward more openness.

When the initial contact is characterized by a clear demonstration that you understand the conflict well enough to successfully restate, in the presence of those on the opposite side of the conflict, their position to their satisfaction, then the initial contact is off to a good start. You do not have to walk a mile in the other person's shoes, but you should know how it would feel.

Be clear about their roles and their power to affect the perceived crisis, as each person has his own conscious and unconscious issues with which to deal. Be clear about the other person's negotiation position and power. It is a waste of time to resolve the conflict at hand by showing all of your views and alternatives if the person on the other side does not have the authority to substantially affect the problem outcome.

Reading the NVL of a lightweight will produce lightweight, ultimately useless data. Choose your audience carefully whenever possible. If the other individual does not have the authority to come to a conclusion about the disputed differences, you need to assess what access he has to the real decision-makers. Kings send out pawns, but are equally defended and represented by them.

Keep in mind that the negotiator's position either may or may not reflect his true feeling in the matter. HINVL factors, cultural biases or the nature of the specific conflict may affect the position taken personally and professionally by the other person with whom you must negotiate.

Even before the meeting officially begins, it can be useful to establish the basic responses of the person with whom you must negotiate. Here are a few suggestions as to how you may gather this data. Relate a story that reflects injustice where anger would be a natural and universal response, and watch his reactions carefully. "Yesterday, when I was shopping with my spouse, someone dented my car and left no note, and the damage was fairly substantial." Test for truthfulness in the other person by asking him whether he would feel angry in that situation. In other words, find examples that elicit basic emotional responses. His responses should sound uncontrived and believable, pure and natural.

I recently returned from central Asia, where the past plagued the present once again. Warring factions with differing beliefs, sharing the same religious concepts, were killing each other over historical disagreements about the translation of the same text. Afghanistan's Taleban, who now control the majority of that country, are potentially threatening the stability of the entire region. When old ideas do not get new thinking, the conflicts of the past thrive in the present. Fears about ideas and ideals limit life in the region. There are serious concerns about the Teleban pushing their extremist, fundamentalist position. The Koran, with its wisdom, written hundreds of years ago, has developed a wide range of interpretation, just as has the Bible. The concern today is the bloodshed over old ideas and present translations. The views about the words of the past are killing some people now. Border skirmishes flare up, and lives are lost when historical points of view collide.

The dilemma that exists is how you negotiate with a group that you do not acknowledge. When governments negotiate with factions from another country they give an implicit credibility and endorsement to those with whom they negotiate. If a regional government is more moderate than the powerful faction which directs and influences a country, there is a national tendency to negotiate with those who have recognized status and a more moderate viewpoint. If, however, those holding a more provocative position are the ones who hold the real power, then those people involved in resolving conflict are faced with a basic question: Am I willing to negotiate with those who say their position is non-negotiable? By definition, those suggesting this hard line, pose the most difficult challenge in resolving conflicts.

In a recent meeting this dilemma became clear once again. I asked the head of the national Security Council about his willingness to negotiate with the Taleban. His answer was ultimately yes, but it was preceded by a series of non-answers, which reflected the difficulty previously mentioned.

Ultimately the negotiation of the non-negotiable is the challenge of the diplomat. This difficulty often shows the difference between a diplomat and a statesman. Bold moves imply risks. Sometimes the pressure of the moment causes difficult decisions to emerge. This is especially true when the media has identified a problem, and presses for an answer. The recent accord achieved in Maryland between the Arabs and Israeli's is a good example of this. The end of the conference was extended day by day until an agreement was reached. The collective pressure to reach agreement forced those who believe that it was impossible to rethink their basic belief. Implicit in this idea is the notion that agreements can be reached when people commit themselves to the idea that communication and conflict resolution is ultimately possible.

Creative problem solving must first be proceeded by creative thinking. Creative thinking in this instance implicitly suggests openness and a willingness to see those positions held by others in a new light. No agreement will last when those making the agreement do not really support it. That is why it is essential to long term success in crisis management and conflict resolution to read the underlying unconscious agenda of those with whom one negotiates.

The negotiator will have to take into serious consideration the depth of belief and commitment to these old ideas if progress is to be made in resolving this dangerous conflict in this region. It could, if not checked, put the world in peril.

Be aware of the NVLs of the other members of the opposite negotiating team. The NVL data should be used to initiate issues. By knowing the other person's NVL-responses to basic emotions such as anger, fear, frustration and surrender, you have the real basis for substantive actions that will last and not unravel later. There is no guarantee that other factors will not alter the outcome of important talks, but you can secure your end of the negotiation by acting on the non-verbal unconscious messages of those across from you.

11 THE META-LEVEL

Meta-level awareness exists when the individual is able to rise above the conflict or crisis and grasp the larger picture as well as its underlying dynamics. Some individuals have a natural ability to stand at a distance, and behave as though they were a third party in a two-party conflict.

The poem, written by Kipling, gives a good definition of meta-level:

If you can keep your head when others are losing theirs and blaming you . . .

It not only suggests not panicking, it also suggests that you look differently at the situation. This is what is meant by getting on a meta level; To look in a different way at those events that overwhelm, confuse or trigger irrational behavior. Meta-level implies the ability to stay grounded in a whirlwind of hostile words. The best test of one's success at achieving this state is by feeling your bodily signs. Tight breathing, sweaty hands, tension in the shoulders, tightness in the throat, and tightness in the stomach all suggest that meta-level is more of a goal than an achieved reality. Meta-level implies that the individual is living in the here and now, that past conflicts are not being projected into the future and destroying the opportunities of the moment.

How does one know if he is living in the here and now? There are a number of indicators.

F eelings are generally more intense.

O ptions are increased as more are perceived.

C oncentration is greater.

U nderstanding of variables is increased.

S enses are heightened, sight, smell, sounds, tastes and touch.

E nergy is more available.

D irection is more obvious and possible.

How do you develop the skills to be here and now? The key to developing those skills is based upon how much insight and awareness a person possesses. This implies an appreciation of, and a motivation toward achieving self-awareness.

I llumination of past unresolved perceived traumatic events.

N otice how much of the day is spent living in or reflecting on the past.

S earch out and deal with obstacles that limit involvement with the present.

I nitiate dialogue with people with whom unresolved issues still exist.

G rasp the importance and impact of the past on the now, and take action.

H eed psychosomatic issues, as past problems are manifested in the body.

T herapy is often the ultimate key to living in the now.

No problem can be solved at the level on which it develops. One must stand back from the arguments, and realize that both sides in any conflict believe that their position is the correct one, the more accurate view of the situation. The negotiator must somehow get above the issues and see them from a fresh perspective. To do so gives him at least four distinct advantages:

The meta-level person, because he is more relaxed in his view of the issues, is less likely to see them in only a two-valued orientation. He will be more apt to recognize shades of gray rather than black versus white, good versus bad or right versus wrong.

The meta-level person is able to absorb more data and introduce it into the process. This, in turn, expands the bases for clearer, longer lasting decision-making.

When we are calm and open to divergent points of view, we can hear and see more, so our decisions are more relevant and accurate.

The opposing parties sense the open mindedness of the meta-level person, and they begin to feel safer and more able to be open, themselves. Just as violence begets violence, sincerity begets trust, the principal component of successful negotiations.

Let's review the concept of meta-level thinking. Its advantages are obvious because it frees us from limited thinking processes, but its attainment is often elusive. The nine-dot problem serves as an example of the value of meta-level thinking. It is said that there are sixteen different ways to solve it. The challenge is to connect the nine dots with four consecutive straight lines without lifting your pencil from the paper.

A hint that may help you solve this problem and others: you cannot solve the problem from within the problem. When you think outside of the nine dots, you are doing meta-level thinking. The solution to this problem can be found on the last page of this book.

THE NINE DOT PROBLEM

12 THE ANATOMY OF CRISIS

If the goal of life is balance, it must follow that whatever creates imbalance in the individual, will create tension, dredging up the ultimate fear: the fear of losing control. In itself, though, conflict is not necessarily crisis; it is merely tension and, as is commonly understood, some tension is not only unavoidable, it is desirable because we need some level of stress to "keep us on our toes." We test ourselves by seeking out competition in business, sports, games, and elsewhere because we enjoy challenge; and challenge generates stress. The difference between a merely stressful situation, an irritation or inconvenience, and a crisis, then, is a matter of degree. A crisis exists when the individual believes that, unless the challenge is successfully and quickly met, "all will be lost." When the individual's unconscious and/or conscious self-concept evaluates a situation as being untenable, too much to handle, beyond his abilities, he is in crisis.

But as devastating as crises may appear to be, they have at least two positive aspects: they force re-evaluation of strategies that had previously been understood to be adequate for dealing with threat, and they offer opportunity for making things better.

The system presented here provides the individual with a method whereby he can expand his own frame of reference, in advance, so that he can approach crises more creatively and enhance the likelihood of achieving successful outcomes.

In general, there are three classes of crises:

Intra-psychic crisis: Within the individual, the conscious and unconscious self-concepts are dominated by unresolved perceived traumatic events (PTEs) from the past. These inner conflicts limit his capacity to evaluate situations accurately and react appropriately.

Interpersonal crisis: Two or more persons hold conflicting perceptions of events, motivations or strategies necessary to clarify, understand or resolve perceived differences or difficulties.

Environmental crisis: Two or more persons hold the perception that their survival or quality of survival is threatened.

To be effective in dealing with each of these three classes of conflict, certain personal characteristics are desirable. They may be recognized, particularly openness to difference, as being life-enhancing qualities in and of themselves, but they are especially significant when dealing with highly emotionally charged situations.

Ideal characteristics for dealing with intra-psychic crises:

■ Openness to difference.

■ Minimum of unresolved PTEs.

■ Creative approach to difficulties.

■ Knowledge of relevant specialties.

■ Action orientation.

Ideal characteristics for dealing with interpersonal crises:

■ Openness to difference.

■ Patience to listen carefully, to withhold judgment until the last possible moment.

■ Creative thinking.

■ The ability to stay focused on the objective.

■ The ability to think on your feet, to interact quickly but not rashly.

Ideal characteristics for dealing with environmental crises:

■ Being a good team player.

■ Openness to input from other disciplines.

■ Knowledge of cross-disciplinary training.

■ Ability to follow command structures.

■ Leadership capabilities.

13 SCIENTIFIC HUMANISM: THE HUMAN ASPECTS OF CRISIS MANAGEMENT

Life is a series of processes which, in spite of our best efforts, we are powerless to completely control. Childhood becomes adolescence, which, in turn, becomes adulthood and, finally, old age. On a personal level, we spend untold billions trying to stop the spinning ball, buying pots of creams that promise to restore lost youth, believing that smooth skin and lots of hair are somehow related to happiness. We look back with nostalgia at the good old days when we had health, vigor and optimism; and we encourage the young to enjoy the moment, because we know it is fleeting and, in time, will become hectic, filled with hassles and headaches.

Of course, only time will determine to what degree our personal processes, our strategies and life-views were effective. In the meantime, we try to manage our ordinary crises as best we can and hope that extraordinary crises – floods, tornadoes, earthquakes, wars and the like – will be managed for us by extraordinary people. For life-threatening events, we look to those we believe to be greater and more powerful than ourselves.

As children, we learned, with our ever increasing acuity, to deal with smaller and then larger issues but, when they were more than we could handle, we went to Mom or Dad whom we considered to be sages and, in most instances, this turned out to be, from our point of view, the correct strategy. They protected us from the dark and the monsters that were hiding in it. We see, though, in retrospect, that most of us, unfortunately, programmed ourselves to seek our parents' answers when the solutions were often readily within our grasp. We were conditioned to look outside ourselves for our solutions.

As a therapist, one of my principal activities has been teaching that, in most cases, the answer to the problem lies within the client. "I will assist you in gaining access to your strengths and competencies," I declare, "so that you can deal with your life's conflicts by yourself with the resources you have."

I am not saying, here, that reaching out is, as many might believe, a sign of weakness; I am merely suggesting that too much of this behavior may simply reflect early childhood experiences that could be playing tricks on us, robbing us of the sheer joy and sense of accomplishment that comes from steering our adult lives. Indeed, after first assessing the situation and reaching inside for the tools and tactics required to deal with it, and finding them wanting, we should never hesitate to reach out. It is the appropriate action.

I admire Churchill because he had the image, and deservedly so, of the kind of person I most respect, a man of self-reliance, leading a defiant nation against a marauder that sought no quarter. Yet even he, in 1941, when he saw that his resources would be unable to withstand the German onslaught, reached out for help. He didn't beg to be rescued; he simply asked President Roosevelt to, "Give us the tools and we will finish the job!"

Churchill was dealing with a crisis, an unprovoked attack. I believe that is the only real crisis there is. The goal, in this situation, cannot be justice; in fact, justice is usually a casualty. The goal is victory.

But there is never an action that is truly unprovoked; it is always motivated. The aggressor is simply unable to communicate his needs in a way that will get them satisfied appropriately. His behavior, all behaviors, exists in some context and, to be understood, it must be assessed within that context even though the understanding does not necessarily excuse the behavior. A criminal is a criminal and, since he did the crime, he must do the time.

All conflict between humans is a communication about a lack of communication. Violent outbursts, then, are, in a sense, justifiable; the aggressor, a person or a nation, perceived the circumstances as being simply irresolvable by any other means. What, then, if anything, does this point of view offer in the way of assistance in dealing more effectively with international crises?

Historically, we have always dealt with them by the same means: war. But my friend, Bill Pemberton, a psychologist committed to searching for the solutions to global conflict, reminded me recently that, "War as a problem-solving strategy is unacceptable when we consider the technological advances we have made in munitions." We need smarter people not just smarter bombs.

14 ORGANIZATIONAL ASPECTS OF CRISIS MANAGEMENT

When trying to evaluate a crisis, there are some critical questions to be asked, as Mitroff and Pearson, in their book on crisis management, suggest:

"1 The range or prior crises that may have given rise to the current one, as well as the range of other crises that may result if the current one is not handled properly.

2 Potential early-warning signs of the crisis, and the status of mechanisms that can prevent or contain it.

3 Factors, technical, human, and organizational, that may cause crises.

4 The parties who may affect or be affected by it."
(Mitroff and Pearson, 1993)

No crisis impacts solo upon one aspect of an organization or a government. There are implications and consequences upon all aspects. The technological factors determine the manner in which data is gathered and processed. The individual human factors are critical because they will be factors in how the crisis is perceived and translated. The organizational and cultural dynamics will result in the organization's or government's response based on organizational goals and cultural values. The image, honor, history and reflection on cultural values will all be factors in governing responses to crises.

Mitroff and Pearson observed:

"Examination of recent organizational crises reveals that they occur because of interactions between three systems: the technological, the individual human, and the organizational/cultural. To be comprehensive, crisis-risk assessments must include the analysis of management priorities for each of these systems and the inactions across all three."
(Mitroff and Pearson, 1993)

> Mitroff and Pearson suggest five system-related components in crises. "Most organizations find it difficult to do well on all five system-related components of a crisis: technology, organizational infrastructure, human factors, organizational culture, and emotions."

The human aspects are perhaps the most important factors in dealing with crisis management. The people responding to the conflict will ultimately determine how the difficulty is perceived and what actions are necessary to take (if any) to correct the difficulty. The governmental structures, like corporate systems, are composed of individuals who will direct the responses.

> "Technical systems neither exist nor operate in a vacuum. In most cases, the cause of a major crisis cannot be traced to the isolated breakdown of a technical system. Rather, crises occur because of the simultaneous breakdown of technical, organizational, and human systems. It makes no sense to analyze the systems comprising an organization's core technology in isolation from the human and organizational system that implement the core technology."

> The innermost layer, the emotional structure of the organization, comprises the emotional responses shaped by senior executives themselves."
>
> (Mitroff and Pearson 1993)

Understanding a crisis is difficult to do while it is evolving. There are usually increasing numbers of people involved as the crisis develops and expands. There is a geometrical progression of issues to be taken into consideration. The issues become more complex as people enter trying to resolve what heretofore had remained a problem.

Perhaps this awareness explains President Kennedy's action in the Cuban missile crisis. A kitchen cabinet is, by definition, smaller than a Department of State. The non-verbal leak was described as a stone hitting a pond radiating its concentric circles. When a crisis is considered on the level of the unconscious meanings to those involved, it is like a handful of stones hitting the pond at once, each having its impact, each with its own epicenter, and each influenced by the other stones hitting the pond of the unconscious.

What does all this have to do with assumptions and CM? Mitroff and Pearson state that:

> "Assumptions embody the presumed properties of stakeholders. In the drug company, the proponents of the different alternatives disagreed because they were assuming very different properties among the stakeholders' behaviors. In regard to CM, the bigger and more complex the crisis, the wider the array of stakeholder forces likely to be involved. As a result, more assumptions will have to be made. In impending crisis, many important facts cannot be known prior to working through the crisis itself. Rather, a clear understanding of the nature of the crisis may only result from working through it."
>
> (Mitroff and Pearson 1993)

A number of things must be taken into consideration when a crisis begins to unfold. Mitrof and Pearson state the following:

> "In the heat of a crisis, a number of the activities must be performed simultaneously, which means that these activities will overlap. During the first few hours (and throughout the first week or even longer), the critical responsibilities of crisis managers will be fact-finding, analysis, damage control, and communication." (Mitroff and Pearson 1993)

The three items that must be addressed are:

One: Analysis. What is happening? How did it happen? Who is responsible? How bad is it? What are the implications and possible consequences?

Two: What can we do? What should we do, and what is the best way to do it?

Three: Whom would we notify first about the crisis? What should we say? With whom should we share this information and who should deliver it?

What to do? The child who learned to turn to his parents to exact revenge on the playmate who took the best toys by force is now a negotiator by profession. He could be Khrushchev pounding his shoe on the desk at the United Nations assembly, Ted Kennedy at Chapaquidick or Wilbur Mills with his Australian firecracker on his arm. The first of these, when he did not get his way, threw a tantrum. The other two simply believed that they were so extraordinary that the rules of decency did not apply to them.

And yet, there are truly extraordinary leaders among us; they just don't want to be associated with the class of leaders we now have. I recently had a discussion with a man who holds a top appointed position in his country's government and who, I believe would make an outstanding President there. I asked him whether he had ever considered a career in politics.

"Absolutely not!" he fired back. "I would never allow my life to be put under a microscope. Would you?"

We were unanimous.

For the past twenty-five years I have lived about half the time in Europe, so I have been given the opportunity of viewing my country, America, from inside and out. I conclude that something is seriously wrong at home. Most disturbing, to me, is the trend for our decision-makers to skirt the hard issues in favor of the more politically correct paths. We are, after all, a nation of immigrants, a pioneering population that has, over the years, developed softness; we have doused the fire in our bellies with Perrier water.

There are steps we can take to put our house in order, but they are difficult steps. Our leaders and we must first learn to manage our personal crises. We must have the courage, boldly and brashly, to speak our minds honestly, risking offending those who disagree; and then we must stand for what we believe is right. Ten steps toward this personal crisis management goal are:

- Crisis management requires the letting go of the past, and choosing to live in the here and now.
- Crisis management requires the viewing of the issues from the meta-level perspective.

- Crisis management requires the letting go of ethno-nationalism, the myths about the culture's subgroups.

- Crisis management requires a genuine desire to communicate clearly.

- Crisis management requires us to seek out all the primary parties and to listen to them.

- Crisis management requires us to remain focused, not to be distracted by extraneous issues.

- Crisis management requires us always to remember that when people are present, communication is possible.

- Finding all the party's non-verbal leaks before the discussions begin enhances crisis management.

- Crisis management requires us to keep in mind that the answer to the problem is often the problem.

- Crisis management requires us to have the skills necessary to restate each party's position to his satisfaction.

The good manager, however, before he steps into the arena, has established certain principles by which he conducts his own life, and these practices are:

- He sets clear boundaries:
  If I cannot trust your "no," I cannot trust your "yes." This is a difficult concept for many people to accept because, for those who were taught to be polite – meaning indirect – it may be difficult to tell it like it is.

- He is in the here and now:
  When fears from the past are projected into the future, they wipe out the present. It is, as we all know, impossible to change the past; we can affect only the events of the present moment. This is not to say that we cannot influence the future and increase the chances for success in it; of course we can. But fears from the past, particularly those

based on PTEs that had dire consequences, become anxieties in the here and now. The individual must learn to re-symbolize the past and see it in new and creative ways, because then he will be much less burdened with anxiety. One of the criteria for mental health is one's ability to truly experience the ups and downs of the moment.

■ He trusts his feelings:
One's perceptions may be inaccurate, but his feelings are never wrong. We are our feelings, and we know what we feel inside ourselves and we are the only ones who can decide whether to express those feelings. If we keep them in, they will turn into resistance, resentment or even, perhaps, rage. They show themselves in our NVLs and our BNVLs, and in psychosomatic ways, and interpersonal and intrapsychic levels.

■ He is willing and able to make contact:
Those who are reluctant to make contact, are usually reluctant for one or both of two reasons: 1) They have had unfortunate, unsuccessful relationship experiences in their pasts, or 2) they are not aware of appropriate ways to reach out to others. Their perception and, therefore their reality is that contact is not possible, at least not for them; but the willingness to risk attempting contact is fundamental to living life fully. They must learn, in therapy or in daily living, that contact is always possible when communication is possible.

■ He is willing to say what he feels:
Telling a person how you truly feel is not unkind; it is showing respect for him. The fact is that, sooner or later, regardless of whether we give expression to our feelings, they will show themselves.

■ He is open to difference:
The principal hurdle we have to overcome in any negotiation is our natural tendency to react

negatively to difference, different ideas, different language patterns, different skin color and so on. Fear of difference creates anxiety, conflict and crisis but, through careful, courageous self-examination, we can overcome it. Change and growth in belief systems are difficult; they may require changing one's friends, his employment and even his religious convictions.

■ He respects himself:
He knows that, if he doesn't, others will follow his lead. For those who have negative self-concepts, looking in the mirror and saying sweet things – the so-called positive affirmations – is not likely to help much, particularly if the low self-image stems from the unconscious self-concept level. They will need professional help. While it is true that the world is what you make it, before you can make it good and positive, you must take responsibility for yourself.

■ He never lies to himself:
He tries to be someone he can like, and he likes himself for making the effort. He knows he has shortcomings even though there will always be some degree of denial of them in his relationship with himself and with others; but these he tries diligently to keep to a minimum.

■ He is who he appears to be, nothing more, nothing less:
Those who try to be someone else, either to impress others or to deny their own realities, ultimately succeed only in complicating their lives and losing contact with themselves, unable to express their feelings genuinely as they experience them.

■ He is his own best friend:
There is such a thing as a sound narcissism, a self-acceptance, and a healthy self-love. It is the ultimate position of strength; it allows one to maintain a basis for compassion, understanding and respect for others, and it is the standard by

which he measures how much he appreciates and accepts his own qualities. As I said earlier, there is no such thing as an international crisis. There is only the playing out of counter productive strategies by individuals who have differences in perceptions, many of which are rooted in faulty perceptions of early childhood experiences; and we, as crisis managers, try to establish solutions to these human problems. The keys to success are our abilities (and willingness) to be open to the other person's message, to really hear what is said and then to reconsider our own position.

15 LEADERSHIP IN CRISIS MANAGEMENT

Today's leaders face dreadful challenges, and every move they make is beamed instantly by satellite to the big screen to be judged by the world. There is no time for contemplation nor room for error. Mistakes destroy lives and plunge liberty and freedom into decay, and replace hopes and dreams with despair.

It is no wonder that persons in charge seek pragmatic advice from all corners, and spend millions on team-building gurus and efficiency experts. But the essential tools for leadership are within them and, once they recognize that, they can nurture them. We have discovered ten areas of understanding that a leader can augment:

- He must understand himself accurately. He must have good insight.

- He must understand the dynamics of his team.
  - ❖ What is the team's feeling tone? Do they joke around with each other much?
  - ❖ How much physical movement is there around and within the work place?
  - ❖ Does the team ever get together socially after work?
  - ❖ Does communication move easily up and down the chain of command?
  - ❖ Are there cliques, "in" groups and "out" groups?
  - ❖ Are there polarization's around individuals or issues?
  - ❖ Are there secret resentments between members of the group?
  - ❖ Does bad news spread through the team as quickly as good news?
  - ❖ Are there changes in the quality or quantity of the work?
  - ❖ Is the feeling tone around the team negative or positive?

The likelihood that these questions can be answered with complete accuracy is remote, but they are critical; they must be asked. A valuable, often overlooked, source of information about the team is the team's secretary.

■ He must understand how he comes across to those outside of his organization. Perception determines reality. The public doesn't see him playing with his children or visiting with his mother or helping with the dishes after dinner so, in the public's reality, those personae don't exist. The public makes its judgments based solely on what they see; and what they see are the NVLs he shows them unconsciously.

So, rather than risk creating distrust by trying to mask his feelings and motives, it is better for him to talk about what he really feels. The results of resolving these messages from the unconscious self-concept are that he will gain respect and credibility, reduce stress and be more effective.

■ He must understand how he comes across in the media, particularly television.

Since network television producers cut and splice videotape into sections they believe will appear more dramatic, it is of the utmost importance to be as media savvy as possible. Interviews are particularly stressful and, as is well known, stress begets regression. It is essential that he avoid slipping into old strategies associated with the unconscious self-concept.

❖ If he doesn't know the answer, he must never lie and say he does. Rather, he should promise to find the answer and get back to the interviewer. Then, do it.

❖ Before starting the interview, he should take three deep breaths and let them out slowly.

❖ He should state each of his main points at least three different ways.

❖ He must keep his breathing slow and deep.

- ❖ Before the interview, he should have a light snack to avoid a growling stomach and the anxiety that goes with it.
- ❖ He should remember that, when his shoulders are elevated, his breathing becomes short and shallow.
- ❖ He should learn to gauge the interviewer's reactions to his answers by observing the interviewer's breathing.
- ❖ Above all, he should never make a promise he can't keep.
- ■ He must understand the parameters of the enterprise, both stated and implied, in which he is engaged.
- ■ He must be able, on a deep level, to read other's true motives.
- ■ He must have a clear understanding of the concept of meta-level thinking.
- ■ He must have a clear understanding of the effect of his family's programming in his thinking.
- ■ He must have a clear understanding of what he needs to do to maintain a winning posture.
- ■ He must have a clear understanding of the price he will pay for victory.

16 TOOLS AND TACTICS FOR LEADERSHIP: A CLOSER LOOK

Someone once said, a leader is a trumpet that does not give an uncertain sound. Leadership is about action, but action without insight leads to chaos. This is surely an uncertain sound. Often the pressure for decisions reflects the stress on the moment. When tension drives decision making, accidents are often the result. Decisions come from the unconscious self-concept and the conscious self-concept based upon how reality is collectively perceived. The need for decisions comes from a perceived state of unrest that can emanate from either self-concept.

Nothing in this world is black or white except black or white, and more than one aspect of the personality is involved in the process of decision making. When the individual aspects of the conscious and unconscious self-concept are examined, there are certain characteristics that distinguish the two components.

When the need for decisions is primarily based upon the conscious self-concept, it tends to be more pragmatic. It is based less on fear, fantasy, or folly. Clear perceptions of the needs and demands of the actual environment are the factors that reflect this level of the decision-making process.

When one is living in the here and now, he not only sees and hears more of what is happening, he is more responsive to the subtle forces that must be seen and acted upon to stay on top of fast moving events.

This means more accurate data and more information for the decision making process. Decisions based upon anxiety most often lead to failure. If knowledge is power, then information is the fuel, and that exists only in the present. Confidence may come from past victories but all victories took place in the present sometime.

There are several aspects that characterize the conscious self-concept:

■ The decision emanates from the here and now.

- They are more clearly understandable to others in terms of logic.
- They will draw less flack than decisions coming from the unconscious self- concept.
- There will be less incongruence between conscious and unconscious self.
- The decision will motivate more from understanding than from corrosive power. Winston Churchill, in 1939, said of Russia what could be said of the unconscious: "It is a riddle wrapped in a mystery inside an enigma." The unconscious is both a powerful and a poor decision-maker. When decisions emanate from deep distortions that lay unchallenged by the light of logic locked in the recesses of the mind, trouble awaits.

Some years ago an official from the Federal Aviation Administration (FAA) investigated an accident. He told of a copilot who was given an instruction by the captain as they rolled down the runway for takeoff.

He said to the copilot, "Takeoff power." So he did and they rolled down to the end of the runway into the waiting fence.

Later the honest but embarrassed number two said, "I had just been in a fight with my wife prior to getting on the plane. I guess I was still thinking of that and wanting to stay in San Francisco and work things out. When the Captain said takeoff power, I guess I somehow misunderstood the instruction."

Fortunately, there were no injuries, except for the copilot's pride and career. He'd heard what he wanted to hear: Stop the plane. Take off power – and go back and work out the trouble you had with your wife.

This is the power of the unconscious. The man was bright and highly trained with many years of flying experience. He and the captain had been flying together for a long time. In the past, takeoff power had always meant, "Give me power to take off." His unconscious self-concept won this day, leaving him and his conscious self-concept literally up against a wall or fence. There are several aspects that characterize the unconscious self-concept.

- The decision emanates from the there and then and not the here and now.
- The questionable logic causes others to respond more to power than persuasion.
- The decision will have anxiety associated with its expression.
- The decision will be observable in an associated non-verbal leak.
- The decision will have a high probability of failure due to its underlying origins.

Even the finest car needs a tune up once in a while and some periodic maintenance. I have spent many hundreds of hours hearing the faulty logic of the very top leaders of governments or industry. The pitch goes something like this, "Look, Barry, when you suggest that I take some time for myself, I promise that I will do it real soon, but I can't, now. I will. You're right. I just can't do it now. Right after this important whatever."

He is deluding himself and lying to me. On some level it is a noble effort. Here is this giant leader who has psychologically lashed himself to the wheel and is fighting to keep the ship of state afloat. He is admired by many. He appears somehow simultaneously both invincible and vulnerable.

He is to be admired and pitied at the same time. There is an unstated thought and fear that is held by those closest to him. How long can he go on like this? They work harder to support his efforts. All fear that day when he fails to answer the call to duty. It has often been my job to brief the irreplaceable leader's replacement.

What causes this terrible, deadly moth and flame dance? The short answer is the narcissism of the leader. He, on an unconscious self-concept level, believes that, if he does not resolve the crisis, nobody will. He is convinced that he holds the answer to the challenges his organization or country faces, and he alone can overcome the problems.

Ask yourself what you would do if you were driving your car, and one of the warning lights on the dashboard lighted up. Would you head for the nearest service station or disregard the light? When I ask this question of top leaders, they look at me like I am some kind of fool or like I'm kidding. Their expression changes when I look at them and say, "Your dashboard is lit up like the 4th of July." They smile or give a nervous laugh and say, "I know, but I can't do it now, but I promise you I will soon."

This is irresponsible short-term thinking and behavior, which reflects a distrust of his fellow team players. There is hope, however, that he will eventually get the message. When he does, the insight comes like a bolt of lighting. It is often called the first heart attack. Unfortunately about 1/3 die during the delivery.

Yet, is it not obviously critical that the leader must have a clear understanding of the dynamics within the team, and to know on whom he can rely and for what? When one buys a candle, he buys it for the light it gives off, not the heat. When he hires an employee or inherits one, just as with the candle, he is looking to see how much light the new team member can shed on the matters at hand. This task must be weighed in relationship to the heat factor. This tacitly suggests that the boss is physically accessible, emotionally present, and able to see the matter as worthwhile.

Perhaps the two most important issues associated with winning strategies are information and timing. There is an expression that says that timing is everything; but timing without good information is just good timing and, by itself, is usually little better than experience, intuition or just plain, dumb luck.

The military talks about intelligence gathering, and they are correct in referring to information as intelligence because information is such an important component in decision making. Information and timing, generated by the leader, who is both guide and cheerleader, must radiate from the core of the organization. When there is dissention within the team, perceptions polarize and positions harden. The hardening subsequently reduces the information flow and affects the timing necessary for bold moves and clear leadership. Timing without information is merely timing. In fact, information, in terms of its importance, overshadows every other component.

17 NEGOTIATIONS USING THE GOODFIELD METHOD: A CASE STUDY

Oftentimes companies, organizations and businesses find themselves locked in litigation. The costs associated with these disagreements are becoming a burden on society. Increasingly, channels outside of the mainstream are being considered as alternatives to resolving these expensive time-consuming legal conflicts. The use of such approaches as Alternative Dispute Resolution is not new in the U.S.A. or Canada, and the concept of bypassing the time and expense of lengthy trials is becoming more appealing to many facing the prospect.

There is an interesting movement currently underway in the United States that involves turning lawyers from adversarial gladiators into cooperative problem solvers. One of the contentions is that the United States has become such a litigious nation that the resulting cost is threatening the international competitiveness of the country's business. With courts jammed and working time lost, new and more effective tools are being sought by attorneys and judges as they seek solution of conflict and unjamming the blocked courts. International conflicts, when litigated by appellate courts or international tribunals, can take years and create untold suffering. It would appear that this problem will only increase with time. An example of an alternative came about in 1994. The dispute at the heart of the case was highly complex, both legally and factually. Filed in several different courts, it involved many corporate and individual parties; and the parties pleaded a great variety of tort and contract claims, from federal securities fraud and RICO violations to wrongful termination and breaches of fiduciary duty.

The plaintiffs were an individual and certain of his various related business associates who had enjoyed close personal and business relationships with the defendant who had formed real estate syndicates over more than a decade. The plaintiff was a former shareholder and sales Vice President of the target defendant company.

The immediate series of events, which eventually led to the filing of the lawsuit, took place around the time of a merger between the corporate defendants. As a shareholder in the company being acquired, the plaintiff approved the merger and profited financially to a high degree, as his shares were bought out at a premium rate.

But shortly after the merger, the plaintiff's economic relationship was terminated even though he had been one of the most significant income producers in the company for years. Moreover, a short time later, the terms of the merger were renegotiated because of a very marked downturn in the financial condition of the acquired company, such that the plaintiffs stock in the acquiring company became significantly devalued.

Further, during the course of the deterioration of the plaintiff's relationships with the defendants, he suffered a heart attack which he later claimed was the product of stress created by their conduct.

The plaintiff's lawsuit sought millions of dollars for breaches of various fiduciary duties, for alleged wrongful termination of his economic relations, and for their allegedly unauthorized renegotiations of the merger.

As discovery progressed, it became clear that great animosity had developed between the parties over a period of years. Plaintiff had become highly embittered and reacted violently to his allegedly wrongful termination and the stock devaluation. The lawsuit seemed as much a vehicle for retribution as it was for economic relief.

Each side's position seemed to be a function of its respective perceptions of each other as evil, dishonest, incompetent and even criminal. Their monetary settlement positions were, consequently, millions of dollars apart.

Indeed, the plaintiff had threatened that, if his demands were not accepted immediately, he would report their alleged misdeeds to civil and criminal authorities. The defendants, who steadfastly denied any culpability, saw this as a wholly unfair tactic and highly inflammatory.

But it was clear that if the plaintiff took such actions, the emotional response by the defendants would have been such that there would have been no turning back, and settlement would have become impossible. The situation was thus critical and called for a new approach.

As one of the defendant's attorneys, Bill Norman, thought that an examination of the plaintiff's emotional and physical illness might shed some objective light on this situation, which seemed to get more complicated and exasperating at each turn.

No one can argue that basic principles of human communication govern us all. When we fail to communicate, things tend to get worse.

There were a number of other issues involved, as well, that had led to animosity and distrust among the plaintiff's former associates and him. The blame game that had been played for several months, had reduced them to being four closed minds each calling the other minds closed.

When I met with the plaintiff, I was immediately struck by his bright, cheerful, and charming demeanor. He was open and eager to try to halt the crazy legal battle creatively. He was just a man fighting for his rights as he saw them.

I suggested that, if the other fellows were as genuinely dedicated to a fair conclusion as he was, and if they were as bright and creative, we might attempt to gather all the parties in a room and negotiate a settlement. It didn't surprise me, when, a few days later, I was notified that they all had accepted my invitation.

I set about the project by meeting with each of the participants privately, and videotaping their NVLs. Each of them expressed what he wanted to say to the plaintiff about his feelings for him. Moreover, they all stressed the anguish the litigation had caused them, and how they sincerely wanted to end the conflict.

Meantime, I read all the books each of them had written; I wanted to know these men's thoughts and feelings as intimately as possible.

I next videotaped Bill presenting the law insofar as it applied to this case, delineating what was possible and what could be accomplished legally. The meta-message here was, "This can be accomplished satisfactorily, here in this room, without further counter suits, by the people involved."

On the day we were all scheduled to gather, I had the plaintiff arrive an hour early so I could play the tape of the other participants for him. I watched his non-verbal reaction to each individual, which gave me a kind of pecking order to use in the forthcoming discussion. Then I asked him to sit in front of the video-camera and make a response to each of the men who was about to arrive.

When we were all assembled, I had them watch each other's presentation. Then I played the plaintiff's message to each of them. As I saw the many hidden agendas, by way of their NVLs, I surfaced those that I believed were appropriate to the day's objectives. I then demonstrated to each of them that, with the information I gathered from their NVLs, I was able to state his unique feelings and thoughts about all the people in the room to his satisfaction. This established my credentials as an objective negotiator.

The remaining hours were spent in exploring the various ways in which communications had broken down, and each of them came to recognize that he was a co-conspirator in the process. As meaningful communication increased, animosity subsided and we were able to move into the legal realm and examine individual issues, and brainstorm our way to practical solutions.

It soon became clear that money was not really at the heart of the dispute; feelings were. Each of them felt he had been injured in some way. The conflict, which had run on for so long, came to an end, and a feeling of deep relief filled the room. Not too surprisingly, considering how creative and energetic these fellows are, a new mutual project had emerged in which they would all be engaged.

When a person is injured, either physically or emotionally, there will be a need to address the damage. This need may be expressed verbally or non-verbally, consciously or unconsciously but, because it is part of the human design to let emotions in and out, it will manifest itself. The parties in this long lawsuit realized that anger begot only more anger, so they were eager, but unable, because none of them, on his own, could achieve a meta-level position, to secure resolution.

The person charged with the leadership role does not have to be a psychotherapist anymore than a driver needs to be an automotive engineer. He must have good ears to enable himself to hear a discordant sound or a feeling tone that does not ring true. Developing the skills to read other people's non-verbal messages is a necessary tool to have as a leader.

The smart person, wanting to make contact with the leader of the organization, is wise to check with the executive secretary first.

The final test of a leader is that he leaves behind in others the conviction and the will to carry on. Basic to this is a clear understanding of how he comes across to those outside of his organization.

I have said that perception determines reality. This is particularly true when it comes to public people. You are how you are seen. Images shrink or grow based on how you come across to others. The controlled aspect is generated from the conscious self-concept. The unconscious self-concept provides the rest, which is more powerful, especially when stress factors are at work.

The non-verbal leak will show ambivalence when it is felt. This need not negate your message if you talk honestly about your reservations. You are showing it on an unconscious level in your NVL. So, rather than build distrust on doubt, talk about what you feel. You will turn distrust into respect and credibility. The result of resolving these messages from the unconscious self-concept will not only mean more effectiveness in the way you come across to others outside the organization; it will also reduce stress and give more fun and enjoyment. After all, isn't that what it is all about?

The leader must have a clear understanding of his image in the media and on television. Thomas Jefferson said, "The press is the best instrument for enlightening the mind of man, and improving him as a rational, moral and social being." Today Jefferson would probably mention women and television also.

For many people, the "press" is primarily television. Television presents images and truth in such a way that, if

*Pr. Wm. Pemberton and Dr. Goodfield
talk during demonstration 1991*

*Soviet soldiers watching one of the first pro Yeltsin
demonstrations 1991.*

Seminar on Human Aspects of Crisis Management 1991

Seminar with USSR 1991 (Deputy Prime Minister Abalkin)

Sub Group meeting re: Baltic Crisis Negotiations 1990

*Baltic Crisis Negotiation with Soviet Officials and Baltic Republics.
Peter Kissing and Eric S. Goodfield filming.*

*Dr. Goodfield and Horse Whisperer Monty Roberts,
the man who listens to horses.*

*Drs Paul Meerts of The Clingendael Institute, Executive Secretary
Leo Verbruggen of NATO and Mort Rosenblum,
Special Correspondent Associated Press 1997*

Dr. Goodfield and Former President Landsbergis

Mort Rosenblum and Dr. Goodfield at NATO

Dr. Goodfield at German Diplomatic Academy 1997

Former President CBS Pictures Mike Levy, Mort Rosenblum and Rex Allen in "Confrontation" about Symuloten Crisis in Lithuania 1996

Sight of Resistance by Lithuanian People –
Goodfield TV interview with Government Official 1996

Dr. Goodfield interviewing then President Brazausks

*Dekanidze alleged Mafia Godfather in TV interview with Dr. Goodfield,
Godfather accompanied by his aids and translators*

Interview with Newspaper Editor of Lithuanian Paper

you are not careful, you could end up believing that they are reality. Perception determines reality, and context determines meaning, as I have already stated earlier. All reporting is filtered perceptions, whether delivered through the observations of a professional person or the objectivity of a lens. We tend to believe technically produced perceptions more than those provided by people because it is easier to convince ourselves that they represent objective reality. The truth is that you cannot really believe that what you see is true.

When pressed, most people know this. However, we forget, when it comes to knowing, that what we see may not be so. Normally we view with eyes that fail to filter. We survive in a sea of stimuli, some floundering more than others do. What is more, we all are contributors.

I recently addressed an international symposium in London called Diplomacy Beyond 2000. Delegates from 180 countries gathered there to discuss this important issue. Our host, the director of The Diplomatic Academy of London, made the following observations that struck a resonant chord in me. He said:

> "Today there is an interconnection of events in a world where everything happens simultaneously. We have a global economy, a global civilization, a global technology, a global communications system and a global environment. However, as exciting as this prospect is, there are major problems. Network television producers cut and splice video footage in the manner they think will have maximum effect in news bytes of 60-second duration. News media such as CNN show events over and over. While clips are broadcast live into living rooms around the world, reporters ask government officials to comment on the situation. The officials are left to comment in a defensive manner. The slightest nuance, gesture, or error on the part of government officials can achieve great significance when taken out of context, and shown over and over to a worldwide audience. As a result, reality is often distorted and, governments find it difficult to present the message or the image they want.

"Marshall McLuhan pointed out in the sixties that "The medium is the message." Although he was referring to the effect that various types of media have on the way that a message is perceived, his words seem to have a different application today. In many cases the information media has gone far beyond covering events, and have set up their own agendas and their own editorializing about events as they occur. They have become the message givers, instead of being the messengers. Television networks have become a factor in international relations."

(Ayad, 1997)

Years ago I was making some observations on behalf of the federal government during a riot. It was late and I was walking alone to my hotel when, all of a sudden, I noticed a police tactical squad confronting some young African Americans. Wanting to see how the incident was being handled, I stood close to the confrontation. A boy, maybe 16, probably younger, was shouting obscenities at a group of police officers standing at parade rest. They stood silently as the crowed jeered and cursed the police. Suddenly television lights lit the dark. The second the lights hit that cursing boy, he changed. Gone were the swear words and racial epithets.

This young man looked directly into the camera and transformed himself into a little civil rights leader. He began to speak; "We demand . . ." "We feel . . ." "We won't. . ." The cameraman changed his position so he and the camera saw the back of the boy facing the police.

There was no doubt about it, this was hot stuff; it was perfect for the 11 o'clock news.

Pushing her way through the crowed of rioters was an old woman. The fearless civil rights leader was grabbed by the ear and pulled through the people as they stood there with shocked expressions!

The amazed crowd watched and listened to the old black lady saying, "Billy Boy, don't you know what time it is? You get your black ass home and into bed right now! Tonight is a school night!" What people watching the 11 o'clock news saw was a noble civil rights leader, confronting an overwhelming police presence. What you see, "Ain't necessarily so."

Those involved in crisis management must take into consideration that what they say to the media can profoundly affect the emotional states of those who are viewers. This has been historically true and is of even more concern as mass media now has the capacity to flash faxes around the world in seconds.

Sjoberg observed that:

> "It is indeed easy to see that people in modern society are deeply concerned about risks. The mass media are full of risk information, and this state of affairs is reasonably seen as a response to demand from their consumers. The coverage was Swedish national politicians tripled the proportion of legislation. One major daily in Stockholm managed to print an initiative concerning risk from the middle of the 1960's to today. (Sjoberg et al, in press)

> But this is not a modern trend: We have studied the intense interest of the mass media in the first major railway accident in Sweden in 1864, some 400 kilometers south of Stockholm (Drottz-Sjoberg & Sjoberg, 1991b; Sjoberg & af Wahlberg, 1996). It is remarkable how fast and extensive the account appeared, as front-page news, the day after the accident. And remember, there were no telephones in those days! The accident also illustrates that accidents have a strange fascination for people even if they are very poor and have to struggle for survival; and in 1864 Sweden was a poor country, indeed.

> Another illustration is provided by a study of contemporary slum dwellers in Sao Paulo, Brazil (Nyland, 1993). They rated a number of risks, and their ratings were compared to many other groups in Europe and the USA. We found that they rated all risks as higher than all other groups we compared to them – and this was true even for esoteric

environmental risks one might have considered irrelevant to people struggling for survival in a dangerous and impoverished environment."

(Sjoberg, 1998)

The competition for stories and material to fill the growing number of channels and networks is terrific. The result is that people in positions of leadership are targets of intense interest and scrutiny to somebody, somewhere.

When something is discovered that is seen as newsworthy about an individual or organization, a fact-finding frenzy begins. What compounds this process is that individual and factional groups see the story as a way to get their positions on television.

Women's groups, ecology groups, conservation groups, gay and lesbian groups, political groups, sub-groups and counter sub-groups look to see if there is something about which they should be taking a position. They want to piggy-back on the story that is currently seen as newsworthy. The leadership role in a major organization requires media savvy. Here are a few things to keep in mind when you are on-camera:

- If you don't know the answer, never lie, and say you do.

- If you don't know the answer to a question say you will find out and get back to them.

- If you say you will get back with an answer, never fail to do it.

- Before starting an interview/news conference, take three deep breaths and let them out slowly.

- When making a main point restate it in at least three different ways.

- Remember to keep your breathing slow and deep during the interview.

- Have a snack to avoid a growling stomach and the anxiety that goes with it.

- When you have your shoulders elevated your breathing gets short and shallow.

■ Watch the interviewer's breathing to gauge the responses he has to your answers.

■ Don't make a promise you can't keep.

Doing a television program is an anxiety-producing event for most everyone. With stress goes regression. The pressure is certainly there to cause a person to slip into old strategies, especially those associated with the unconscious self-concept. What can be expected is that everyone involved will show the NVLs more intensely. The best policy a person can follow in this situation is to follow the suggestions just given. It may also be helpful to role-play the news conference or interview with your staff.

In trainings that we offer, we stage a mock news conference, and a crisis scenario that is specific, realistic and tailored to that leader's particular area of operation. What happens in these situations is that the participants learn in an intense encounter. They work with a top journalist on how they come across. The whole interview is done with professional cameras and closed circuit video. After the news conference, an intensive review takes place.

There are two aspects:

■ Technical media tips based upon their performance.

■ The training begins when all staff leaves and I give personal feedback.

My experience, doing this with world leaders, is that, even though they do television virtually every day of their lives, they are still surprised and grateful for the chance to receive this kind of information. It seems that it is possible to reach a position where real, honest, useful and new information is available. It is a paradox that, where information is most necessary, it is often most absent.

Another aspect of these training's is focused on individual instruction in learning to read other people's NVLs. Many of these individuals, with whom they interact, are public officials, and they, too, are on television regularly. This provides a unique opportunity to examine, on an NVL level, someone whom they meet across conference tables regularly.

The leader who finds him or herself on television, is what the viewer sees as his reality, just as the viewers watching the little civil rights leader saw reality.

Although your image begins in a television studio it will end up in a little box in somebody's home or office. Never forget this!

One must have a clear understanding of the rules of the game, stated and implicit. No leader ever reached a real position of power without mastering this skill to some degree. There are a lot of sharks in the water these days.

This is nothing new, but there seems to be a new breed I call the stealth shark. This nasty thing can pass himself off as a guppy or gold fish.

Basically there is no need to discuss the stated rules of the game other than to point up the obvious. The old expression holds true: The only thing that does not change is change. Nothing has changed regarding that remark.

Power is like money. How much is enough? Just a little bit more. The top leader can go to sleep at night knowing that someone, somewhere is dreaming of his job, and how it would be done better if they were doing it.

Whether it be a board of directors or the people of a country, we all answer to somebody. We are concerned with two primary issues:

1. How can we anticipate the needs and demands of others?

2. How can we get our needs met?

There are numerous subcategories but these are the main ones.

Understanding and surfacing the hidden agendas of those with whom you must work is not easy. Some people say that they use intuition. I was taught that intuition was really a series of sub-verbal cues, immediate perceptions, or judgments made without any mental steps in preparation. Now, when someone says that, I think more than likely he is picking up on the non-verbal leak of the person. What is certain is that we feel more comfortable around some people than we do around others. There are reasons for this, of course, such as issues of values and views and strategies. Many of these factors can be assessed on a non-verbal level.

One must have a clear understanding of how to read other's deepest motivations. In order to get a clear picture of these factors that affect the motivations, we need to consider the issues that affect congruence in verbal and non-verbal messages.

- The merits of what we are asserting.

- The role of our own personal history in any given communication.

- The nature of the personal history.

- The degree of conflict resulting in PTEs on an unconscious level.

- The emotional state of the person now.

- The unconscious motivation in saying what we say.

- The degree that what we are saying conflicts with the conscious or unconscious.

- The degree of outside pressure from others as we attempt to communicate.

- The amount of generalized stress that we carry.

- The degree to which we are unconsciously trying to mislead another.

It is obvious that, in intense or crisis communication situations, there are many things to consider. The two most important are what is going on in you and what is going on in the other person. There are four other issues to consider when trying to assess motivation: The conscious, the unconscious, the verbal message, and the non-verbal message.

The individual, who develops skill in these areas, not only will become a better leader, but will also become a better and more successful person.

In general it is good to remember that your system is constantly communicating what is going on inside you. The more you try to control, deny or block the expression of what you really feel, the more you will leak the emotion in another part of your system.

Here are factors to consider when communicating. They should be general principles by which you monitor yourself and evaluate the actions of others.

Talk about what you feel; it shows anyway. Credibility increases when you talk about the obvious. It would be silly to pretend that you feel happy or alert with something when you are sending an absolutely different non-verbal message. Remember the last time you were in a fight with a loved one, and he or she said, "Let's go and see this movie." You really did not want to go but you said, "It is okay with me. I'll do whatever you want!" At the same time you are saying yes, you are making a face as if somebody is pulling out one of your front teeth.

At the same moment, your loving partner is saying, "Okay, if you are going to be like that, I don't want to go anywhere!" Here is an example of the proper use of sending a clearly incongruent message to achieve an objective. Generally, however, if you want to keep your credibility, and have people see you as clear and congruent, do not do this.

Be aware of breathing, as it communicates the general levels of tension in the system. All parts of our systems breathe and, therefore, all parts of the body are communicating the general state of the system. This data is picked up by people on different levels of awareness. This information can be useful, and should be a regularly used tool in your data-gathering arsenal.

Be aware of tension pulsing in the jaw. It relates to unexpressed aggression. Perhaps one of the most obvious predictors of unexpressed anger is when the masseter muscle begins to pulse. It quite literally reflects a process when someone is exerting pressure by biting down on his own teeth. When you see this, you can be sure of two things.

The first is that this more than likely reflects a long-standing strategy of blocking the normal expression of aggressive feelings. This can be determined by looking to see if there is a build-up or oversized muscle development in the jaw. Another indicator is a long-standing strategy of difficulty in expressing anger. Look at the teeth. If you notice that the teeth look as if they are ground down from what dentists call clenching, then you can be sure that this person has a need to block the expression of the aggression that he feels when he feels it.

What you are seeing now that is incongruent with what is being said may indicate a clicking or denial of the deeper unconscious message.

Assuming that everything is A-OK, this is another technique that will provide a wealth of specific data. It's simple. Every time that you see the person take a breath, you do exactly the same. There are two factors to be considered here, rate and depth.

The rate is the speed at which a person breathes in and out. The depth is how much oxygen the individual takes in and lets out. What will happen is that, in less than a minute, you will be experiencing that person's emotions. You will have matched the two respiratory systems. This means that, if he is feeling anxiety, so will you. And if he is feeling, calm and relaxed, you will feel the same emotion. First impressions are important. Knowing what the other is feeling, before you begin, can be useful, especially when it is based on fact.

What this exercise will not provide is an explanation of why this person is experiencing this particular emotion. What you will have, however, is an edge on the other person. The encounter begins with you having hard data before the first shot has been fired.

Shortening or lengthening sentences changes tension by altering blood chemistry. Some years ago I taught hostage negotiation techniques to law enforcement officials who might find themselves trying to resolve a hostage situation.

In this particular approach we use the breathing not just for diagnosis; we use it to actually intervene, and alter the behavior itself. Most terrorists or hostage takers are not dealt with on a face-to-face basis. The telephone is the primary method of communication. The first moments are among the most critical. Often they have followed an act of violence and murder. At this point, the hostage taker is most unstable and dangerous. The negotiator who is involved with finding a way out of this situation needs to achieve two conditions immediately: He must calm the suspect to reduce the possibility of further uproar, and he needs intelligence based on good information.

This can be particularly difficult when, as is often the case, the perpetrator is shouting and swearing, yelling unrealistic demands into your ear on the phone. The question is how to calm someone and alter his or her perspective on the issue. Here is how to do it. I explain this technique so you can adapt it to your particular circumstances. I hope that they never involve terrorists or other crazy folks. Often we are confronted with what we refer to as people who are experiencing an aroused state of the organism. Sometimes the organism can get so aroused that you think that the phone could explode in your face.

If you need to cool things down, here is a way to do it. Regardless of whether the person is on the phone or standing in front of you yelling in your face, do this:

Bring your voice up to the level of the other person's. Notice the length of sentences being spoken.

Usually in crisis, they are very short and on a high order of abstraction. That means that they leave out a lot of information. An example is talking about office equipment vs. talking about pencils, which can also be seen as office equipment.

When you respond, make your sentences just a little longer than the other person's. This will start to get more oxygen into the bloodstream of the upset person. By doing this, you restore balance to the blood chemistry. This is necessary if the person is to feel calmer.

Start to lower your voice, at first a little at a time. This is pacing. Do not go too fast. Pace him, and let him be your guide. Start to lengthen your sentences more and more. What you are doing here is altering his breathing pattern. At this point you are about to get the lion back into his cage. Obviously your motivation and meta-level is important here.

Flutter rate or blinking speed gives important data. The more anxious a person becomes, the more his flutter rate will increase. This long known fact forms the basis for the importance of rapid blinking and its relationship to a clear understanding of behavior on a deep level. Usually it is paired with rapid eye movement, referred to by researchers in this area as REM. When this state is noticeable in someone, it exists as a result of a perceived threat to that person's self-concept. This perceived threat can exist on either level of consciousness. When it is the result of a perceived threat to the unconscious self-concept, the higher flutter rate will be the more chronic state of the person. This is because the person has surfaced, to a more conscious level, an unresolved perceived traumatic event (PTE) from his past. It has, for some reason, like an old injury that one feels in cold weather, reactivated to remind the person of the past injury.

Again, as a result of this knowledge, you have a choice. In some cases it may be necessary or desirable, to let the anxiety exist for some period of time. When a slow flutter rate is seen, it reflects a state of calm. Again this information will give you a chance to evaluate those around you.

When tension builds in the body, it can be increased or decreased via movement. The body becomes fatigued when it remains docile too long. When in a conference, negotiation, or a long board meeting, it is necessary and appropriate to have movement of some kind, an activity that changes the feeling tone of those in the gathering. When there are stress factors associated with the meeting, this is particularly true. Lack of movement results in reduced concentration, creativity, and interest. Some people are fans of long argumentative meetings to browbeat individuals into consent, but this is a formula for unstable agreements and building distrust and resentment. Whenever possible, a more civilized approach is better. Not only will it be more effective, it will generate more goodwill.

The more white that is showing under the eyes, the more there is trance. The eyes are the closest connection to the brain. When the eyes are elevated, the individual is in an altered state of consciousness. Consequently the person is less in the here and now. He is physically present but psychologically absent. It is normal for us to vary our levels of consciousness throughout the day. Obviously there are a number of influences such as how much rest you had, the time of the day, and other issues that are on your mind. When the individual is not in the present, this is no time to present a main point.

There are two different factors to determine. Is this temporary or is it a chronic state with this person? When an altered state is chronic, the person tends to be absent in his dealing with others. This way of relating leads to a vagueness in the decision-making process. This behavior reflects more of a personality type than a unique response to everyday events. When there is white under the eyes and it is a reaction to the moment, it basically means that the person has seen fit to remove himself from the situation. There are a few people whom I have seen who have whites that show on the tops of their eyes. This is rare and it also reflects distancing oneself. I have seen this only a very few times in all the years since I developed the concept of the NVL. The ability to determine this information will save the busy leader time and money.

The tongue coming out regularly is an indicator of aggression. Have you ever had the experience of buying a certain type of car and, when you did, all of a sudden it seemed like they were everywhere and everyone had one? This is how it is with regard to learning about people putting their tongues out as part of a NVL. This response is not uncommon. It reflects the pressure from the unconscious self-concept. The pressure is based upon an unconscious need to express unresolved aggression stemming from a PTE. What is important to note, when you see this, is the frequency and when and what factors influence the rate at which it happens. What you can be sure of is that stress will be an important variable in its expression.

Here is a good source of information but it is necessary to establish a base line first. Of course, when the underlying causality is explored in a therapeutic environment, it is possible to stop this NVL. This is desirable in that the response reflects an unresolved problem. When it is explored and resolved, the person will be more efficient due to the general reduction of stress in the system.

When the tongue comes out regularly and the eyes close directly after, it reflects denial. With most people, when they try to deceive or lie to someone, not only do their eyes blink quickly; their eyes tend to close directly after they state the falsehood. The closing of the eyes takes place within two or three seconds at most. The exception to this rule is the psychopath who has a poorly developed superego and therefore does not experience anxiety when he lies.

This aspect of an NVL is perhaps one of the most important because it reflects the true non-verbal reality. What that reality is saying is that what I am telling you verbally is not the truth as I honestly perceive it. Naturally, this is critical information to have. In order to get a true reading, to know if this is the correct interpretation of the non-verbal behavior, you need to restate the question that first elicited the eyes closing.

This should be done at least three different times throughout the conversation in a non-threatening manner.

The restatement should be done in different ways. For example, "You said that you had nothing to do with X happening. Is that correct?" Later in the conversation, you might say something like, "I know that you had nothing to do with X happening. Right?" You could also say something like, "I know that you were against X taking place. Correct?" We all blink. It is an automatic response we all have. What we do not all have, however, is the need to close our eyes every time a certain word is said. I have often seen in a marriage-counseling situation, a husband or wife close his or her eyes every time he or she says, "I love you." These are the moments when my video equipment is worth its weight in gold, assuming that I was clever enough to turn it on.

Needless to say this is shocking information for all parties involved as the unconscious truth reflecting the ambivalence comes to the surface. The key to using this information is to remember that it is not important data unless it happens every time.

If there is one thing that a person in a position of power must know and not forget, it is that no problem can be resolved on the level at which it develops. This principle is essential to understand and equally important to remember. The leaders of today must deal more quickly and more accurately, using the proper blend of fun and polite persuasion. This tricky tightrope walk is made even more dangerous by the shoot-from-the-hip reactions of others in power positions.

It is not easy to maintain a global perspective when the world via the media pushes for a quick sound bite answer to complex issues. Moreover, the temptation to meet irrationality with more of the same is a hard temptation to overcome.

S. I. Hayakawa used to say to me, "Barry, when tempted to fight fire with fire, remember that firemen usually use water." It is difficult to maintain a sense of calm in the face of dastardly acts and irrational behavior, especially when your reaction is considered newsworthy, and there are cameras in your face.

In the late 60's, Hayakawa was President of San Francisco State College where the biggest, longest lasting student riots took place. At times there were 600 police officers against 13,000 angry demonstrating students. I held the position of Assistant Executive Vice President. I was in charge of the disciplinary hearings.

One day I was officially observing a riot at very close range. There were police lined up at attention, students and outside agitators throwing rocks and shouting obscenities. The tension was high as tempers flared.

I looked into the faces of many of the officers. Behind the shielded, helmeted, protective cover lay the grimaced faced persona of professionals. Darwin said that the goal of life is self-preservation. It is unnatural to stand in front of an unruly mob hurling missiles, and not run or strike out in anger. It was their self-concept and the meta-level awareness that enabled them to accept and survive the onslaught. I must say that I was very happy not to be bound by such restraints. I ran!

The leader of today, metaphorically and, unfortunately, sometimes not so metaphorically, is standing on the front lines leading his troops. It takes more than courage and tenacity to survive and flourish; it takes meta-level thinking and strategies. What exactly is meta-level thinking? It is basically about achieving a global view of an issue or behavior.

Meta-level thinking is the ability to circumvent small and limited thinking processes. When a problem occurs, there is a general tendency to assume that the answer to the problem lies in front of you when much of the time it lies in a special kind of thinking. It is qualitative and not quantitative.

Here is an example of outside-of-the-nine-dot thinking that perhaps saved our world from nuclear devastation. It happened in the final days of the Cuban missile crisis.

President John F. Kennedy reacted, in the fall of 1962, when the Soviets moved offensive weapons, including ballistic missiles into Cuba. The world was faced with what many people felt was the greatest danger of a catastrophic war since the advent of the nuclear age.

Secretary of Defense, Robert S. McNamara, Attorney General Robert F. Kennedy and a few men close to the President, gathered together to try to pull us back from the brink of nuclear annihilation.

The Congressional Quarterly reported that Chairman Khrushchev, on October 26, sent two contradictory letters to President Kennedy. The first, not made public, apparently took the soft line that Russia would remove its missiles from Cuba in return for the U.S. quarantine and assurances that the U.S. would not invade Cuba. The second took a harder line seeking the removal of U.S. missiles from Turkey in return for Russian missiles out of Cuba.

Secretary of Defense McNamara, in the introduction to Robert Kennedy's book on the crisis, titled Thirteen Days, stated that, "He (the President) understood then as now, that, above all else, a U.S. President must, while defending our vital interests, prevent the confrontations between nuclear powers which can lead to nuclear holocaust." He continued saying: "His objective was to force the missiles out of Cuba without war. That objective was accomplished by a strategy which he helped shape and which his brother directed, a strategy which applied pressure against the Soviets without ever pushing them to the point where they were forced to an irrational, suicidal, spasm response."

Here we see the outside-of-the-nine-dots thinking as McNamara describes Robert Kennedy's role in the affair: "He showed a shrewd sense of diplomacy both in the concept and in the application of the strategy. As a matter of fact, it was Robert Kennedy's suggestion, when we received two contradictory messages from Khrushchev, the first favorable and the second unfavorable, that we reply to the first and not the second.

He actually drafted the reply, stating the terms we were willing to accept, plucking them from the several often-disparate Soviet messages. They were the terms on which the settlement ultimately was based." On October 28, 1962, President Kennedy fired back this response to the first message:

"I welcome Chairman Khrushchev's statesmanlike decision to stop building bases in Cuba, dismantling offensive weapons and returning them to the Soviet Union under United Nations verification. This is an important and constructive contribution to peace."

Linear thinking, lacking boldness and brains, would have resulted in a far different outcome, one that could have cancelled the rest of the century.

W. T. Sherman, the American Civil War General said, "Courage is a perfect sensibility of the measure of danger, and a mental willingness to endure it." There was something more than endurance that brought an end to the crisis, it seems to me. The State Department would surely not have taken this tack. The idea was bold and creative and, moreover, it worked!

Bob Kennedy used to make this remark as I recall: "Some people look at things and say, "Why?" I look at things and say, "Why not?" Why not say, "Why not?"

This simple concept opens doors, and gives the prospect of another perspective. My definition of creativity is: the ability to hold off judgment until the last possible moment. It means, let everything come in, every idea and thought, regardless of what it says and what it is, or from whom it comes. Then, when the ideas are there, the information gathered can enable one to do three things: organize, fight, and win!

This is the kind of logic that I was fortunately able to witness for a short time from April 4th to June 5th of 1968. I was an assistant to then California State Senator Mervyn M. Dymally, and was assigned to aid Senator Robert Kennedy in his campaign for the presidency of the United States. Bob Kennedy was able to blend his clear thinking with good judgment and empathic feelings. He was truly a person to behold in those high pressured days as he made decision after decision on what he hoped would be the road to the White House.

Additionally, a leader must have a clear understanding of the role of the family.

My promises are simple. All relationships are always either getting better or worse.

Life is compromise, choices, doubt and decision. Having been a psychotherapist, consultant and advisor on three continents for thirty years, this is what my journey has taught me.

I am sure of a few other things too: family plays an increasingly important role as one gets older. When people are dying and they look back on their lives, they don't regret so much what they did, but what they did not do. G L. Banks said in his poem, My Aims:

> I live for those who love me,
> For those who know me true,
> For the heaven that smiles above me,
> And awaits my spirit too,
> For the cause that lacks assistance,
> For the wrong that needs resistance,
> For the future in distance,
> And good that I can do.

The decision-makers who direct and guide our lives are often the victims of their own successful lifestyles. Time is the most precious commodity. There is never enough of it and what exists is in dwindling supply.

New technologies trap, not free the roadweary executive. Long electronic tails wrap around these leaders as they struggle for moments free of demand. Automobiles speed down the road, going God knows where, filled with car phone conversation that apparently is so important that it must take place now.

Now there is e-mail, tomorrow X, Y and Z- mail. All of which give information.

When the data produced is considered in relationship to the relevant knowledge it provides, it is more than likely a waste of precious time. There appears to be confusion between information and knowledge. "Knowledge is power," said Francis Bacon, in his Sacred Meditations. If knowledge is power, there is a growing energy crisis, and our families are suffering.

I know NATO's Secretary General Javier Solana. The grueling schedule that he keeps is truly remarkable. He is a man of extraordinary charm and great personal energy. His official residence is in Brussels; however; his wife, who is also a professional, lives in another country with the family. They visit regularly, commuting between countries and pressing engagements.

This trying lifestyle is not unique when it comes to many corporate and government leaders. As I said, life's a compromise. Our society sanctions wives and husbands being apart from each other and the family when it is on business.

What happens, however, is that there is an ability to adapt to this emotionally taxing and potentially dangerous situation. That is the good news and it is the bad news.

When this lifestyle's price becomes too high, all involved end up paying. Of this there is no doubt. Let us examine a few questions.

- ■ What are the interpersonal issues that face a top executive today?

- What practical alternatives exist for the person in a position of power?

Accidents happen more often when you live your life in the fast lane, but they can be avoided. You just have to keep your eyes on the goals and on the direction of the road. Oftentimes there is another person involved between the executive and the family. She or he is the Executive Secretary who is charged with many of the detailed dynamics that keep the family together and the executive on the road.

There are two issues that must be assessed: the problems faced and the symptoms of those problems when life in the fast lane starts to get out of control. The pressures of leadership do not represent a unique set of needs. The issues, needs and demands remain the same. From basic survival needs to more complex issues of self-actualization, we are all in the same boat.

What is perhaps special about people in power is the manner in which the needs are met. There must be special systems of contact and communication established lest there be a system crash. Mater atrium necessitous or necessity is the mother of invention.

The Problems:

- How to maintain contact.
- How to maintain quality.

The Symptoms:

- Difficulties on an intra-psychic level.
- Difficulties on an interpersonal level.

As I stated earlier, all relationships are either improving or getting worse. Some people may deceive themselves into believing that things remain in a kind of status quo. This thought usually is self-serving or based upon ignorance. When it is self-serving, it is usually based upon a need to deny a situation that requires a re-evaluation of the current arrangement or lifestyle. This situation is more problematic and, when not dealt with promptly, may result in a complete collapse of the relationship, preceded by bickering, defensiveness, denial and self-recrimination.

When it is based upon ignorance, it is less of a systemic issue. Ignorance is resolvable with information. There will be trouble when the spouse is seen as an acquisition and a done deal.

There is always a problem when a person is seen and treated as an object. This problem usually is symptomatic of a PTE on the unconscious self-concept level. This may reflect contact and intimacy difficulties. It may reflect a systematic way of relating developed in early childhood when the latter is the case.

Counseling couples with individual therapy will be required to sort out the relationship and the underlying causality. Do not put it off because the problem will not go away.

Nobody can justify, rationalize or find an excuse that is more understandable and realistic than the person with major corporate or governmental responsibilities. When there is a division of labor and a tacit agreement about the availability and duties of each member of the couple, a kind of contract-within-a-larger-contract exists.

A person's credibility is of equal importance at home or at work. The adage with which I was raised was that a person is as good as his word. This is still the way I see it.

Children are often the best source of feedback in this regard. After hearing, "I'll be at the game on Saturday," too many times and you fail to show up, they may not say anything, but their feelings about the issue will be as obvious as the scoreboard at the ballpark.

There are often periods of increased activity requiring time away or long hours. The leader needs to honor the contract at home or modify it so that his credibility will remain intact. By doing this, he will reduce feelings of anxiety, guilt, and self-recrimination. The obvious benefit is that he will not be looking metaphorically over his shoulder toward home. The key to success in this area, as well as in all others, is to have respect and clear contracts. The job of leadership is often like a wedge between family, friends and other loved ones. It is imperative that those in positions of leadership maintain their bases of security and support. This is most effectively done when one holds those who are important to him in an active position rather than a symbolic one in his daily life. The answer here is simple. How do you maintain quality in your car or other special possession? Quality controlled maintenance. Even the finest, most accurate rocket requires a mid-course correction, so why wouldn't a long-term relationship? A midcourse correction and check-up can be as painless as a night out together. When this is done, make sure it is just the two of you.

On most all levels, we are ambivalent about our actions. Life's issues are rarely just black or white. There are always consequences for our important decisions. As I said in my introduction, when you go somewhere, you leave somewhere. Sometimes, what we leave behind turns out to be far more important than that for which we left. Those pressed to make these daily decisions would do well to remember.

With regard to the symptoms, there are a number of classic signs of difficulty when a relationship is driving you out of your mind. Difficulty in concentration, headaches and generally any psychosomatic complaint could be manifested. When stress is chronic, it is often caused by a combination of environmental factors occurring now, and factors associated with unresolved perceived traumatic events that are stimulated by the issues occurring in the present day. Stress can be increased by difficulties within the family, and exacerbated by issues facing the leader in the work environment.

Alcoholism and the use of prescription and nonprescription medications are often found as the leader seeks relief from the woes at home. This is common in Eastern and Central Europe, as excessive drinking has been honed to almost a science or art form. There are some leaders who must be seen early in the day if one is interested in a productive and sober dialogue. Another alternative to dealing with the troubles that await the leader is to find a soft shoulder and a hard bed.

How do you maintain a clear understanding of what you need to do to maintain a winning posture? The short answer is Balance, Balance and Balance. To the extent that compromise is a factor in most human interactions, it is necessary to attempt to strike a balance between the duties of office and the needs and demands of one's own familial responsibilities. The leader must give constant scrutiny to the bottom line at home and at work.

The fact that he occupies the position that he currently holds suggests that he is doing something right. Therefore, the concern must be how to continue this winning strategy.

The first thing to do is to assess our perception of how winning the strategy really is. Clear and accurate information should be developed about your position at home just as it is in the workplace. Crisis can be avoided and contact improved when accurate information characterises our relationships with the important people in our lives. Some years ago I developed a test to surface a person's place within his or her interpersonal relationship. Perhaps a good way to avoid conflict would be to take this informative test with your partner, find a quiet place where you will not be disturbed, and follow the instructions exactly. Each person is to take approximately five minutes per section. Do not discuss your responses until you and your partner have both completed all of your **GIVE**. Upon completion, exchange papers with your partner and systematically discuss each section before proceeding to the next one.

Remember, risk taking is in direct proportion to growth. Also be clear that you are showing concern about the relationship by participating in this exercise. Moreover, you are communicating about what both of you see as being important now. That may be all it will take to make a good relationship even better, or to put a troubled one back on course.

GOODFIELD INTERPERSONAL VALUES EXERCISE

SECTION ONE

Write 10 sentences that reflect the main goals you have now and hope to achieve within the next five years.

SECTION TWO

Write 10 sentences that begin with the words, "I am..."

SECTION THREE

Write 10 sentences that begin with the words, "I need..."

SECTION FOUR

Write 10 sentences that begin with the words, "I am concerned (or anxious) about..."

SECTION FIVE

Repeat sections one through four, responding this time as you feel your partner would respond.

SECTION SIX

Rank in order or priority all 10 sentences in all of the sections. Most important will be 1, second most important is 2, and so on.

SECTION SEVEN

Look at each section; write one sentence for each section that captures the feeling tone of each section.

SECTION EIGHT

Look at the four sentences about yourself that you have just written in section seven, and the four sentences you have just written about your partner in section seven, synthesis the four sentences about yourself and the four sentences about your partner into two sentences.

SECTION NINE

Exchange papers and discuss one section at a time, starting with section one and work forward.

SECTION TEN

When participating in this exercise, keep in mind that the goal – as it is in life – is the process and not the end result.

Perhaps one of the most difficult challenges is to keep the lines of communication open at home and work. I know many top leaders who fight for democracy but would never stoop to practising it.

Benito Mussolini, in his book, Fascism, said, "Democracy is a kingless regime infested by many kings who are sometimes more exclusive, tyrannical and destructive than one, if he be a tyrant." Crisis management begins at home, for if the leader lives in an unstable environment, he will bring that to any crisis in his professional life. As stated earlier, the goal of life is balance. It is possible to maintain balance at work when there is imbalance at home, but not for long. It is only a question of time before personal imbalances, whether they be intrapsychic or interpersonal, will impact the performance in the professional arena.

The leader himself in any crisis management circumstance is the most important tool to resolution of conflict. Therefore the fewer crises he carries in his daily life, the more effective he will be in handling his professional responsibilities. Stated simply, if a crisis or conflict exists at home, do something about it; don't put it off. I have seen some Boards of Directors meetings that would make Hitler's tirades at Wolf's Lair seem like nap time at a Montessori school.

The leader would serve his cause well if he would avoid surrounding himself with yes men. Positions of power can intimidate to the point that executive assistants and close colleagues are reluctant to be the bearers of bad news. They may feel the need to protect the leader from difficulties and potential dangers. This is tantamount to covering a driver's eyes on a curvy road because the road might frighten him.

The lifeblood of any person in power is clear, honest information. Sometimes it is a good idea to risk stating the obvious to reiterate the point. The good leader has a clear understanding of the price he is willing to pay for victory.

A major contributor to our demise is our life style choices. There is a price tag on all of our actions. That price tag is called stress. No discussion of world leadership would be complete without mentioning the price paid by all leaders, and that is the role of stress on daily life. It is true; some folks thrive on stress.

Take for instance my life-long friend, Mort Rosenblum, the Associated Press Special Correspondent and former Editor and Chief of The International Herald Tribune. He is a genius wrapped around a reporter's notebook, clutching an old silver Parker pen layered in stress. I once said to him that he should be careful because he was burning the candle at both ends. He called me back a few days later to respond to my concern. "Hey man, it's me. Thought about what you said. I'm working on a new way to burn that candle from the middle." That was 25 years ago, and his flame is still burning brighter than ever.

Stress, according to Hans Selye, the foremost expert on the subject, defined it as: "The body's non-specific response to any demand placed on it, whether that demand is pleasant or not. Sitting in heavy traffic or receiving a lover's kiss may be stressful. Stress therefore, is not necessarily bad. It is not only impossible to avoid stress; it is not desirable."

A certain level of stress is necessary and desirable to grow and flourish, but we need to learn to recognize and effectively deal with stress in our systems. Stress is perceived personal pressure that exists on a psycho-physiological level within the body. Our early decisions regarding perceived personal pressure, coupled with the building blocks of the unconscious self-concept – that is, perceived traumatic events (PTE) – form the bases for strategies that we use now to deal with stress. The roots of our actions now grew out of our pasts. It certainly is a factor in why and how the leader became a leader.

We are oftentimes not aware of what this strategy is or what our personal limitations are when we go beyond our personal stress boundaries. What are the alternatives to overwhelming stress? There are four classic solutions to stress: chemical, physical manipulation of the body, environmental change, and psychological change.

The chemical alternative involves the use of legal or illegal substances, in moderation or excess, by prescription or self-medication. Manual or physical manipulation of the body represents an attempt to break the stress cycle, the body's tendency to generate more stress. Amateurs and professionals alike, with varying degrees of success, practice it. Changing the environment to reduce stress has many forms ranging from moving furniture to moving people.

Psychological change may range from country walks to years on your back on a psychoanalyst's couch. The physical affects the psychological and vice versa. By altering the system psychologically, the physical can also be profoundly influenced. This is most effectively achieved by altering the level of consciousness. It is a quick alternative to carrying stress around in your body. It is easy to do and does not require another person. It is legal and requires no prescription and, finally, you carry a lifelong supply in your system. Let us try an experiment.

■ Get some privacy. You will need about 5 undisturbed minutes.

■ Relax comfortably in a chair. Do not cross your legs. Loosen any tight articles of clothing.

■ Bring your eyeballs up to the top of your head and hold them there. They may flutter.

■ Slowly close your eyelids while still keeping your eyeballs elevated.

■ You may feel some strain in your eyes, and your eyelids fluttering. It is a good sign.

■ You will feel your breathing change because of a change in the metabolic process.

■ Take a deep breath and continue deep slow breathing.

■ Give yourself the suggestion that each breath that you take will let more stress out.

■ Recall a time and place where you felt calm and relaxed or find one in the future.

■ After about 5 minutes, count from 1 to 3. Open your eyes alert, refreshed and awake.

This little exercise can be repeated a few times a day as needed or at night to deepen your sleep, which will also help to minimize and reduce daily stress. Should you choose to add this tool to better deal with the challenges faced as a person in a leadership role, you will not be alone. I personally have shared this tool with many other people, some of whom are heads of state.

18 PERSONAL REFLECTIONS ON THE HUMAN ASPECTS OF INTERNATIONAL CRISIS MANAGEMENT: WONDERINGS AND WAR STORIES

Churchill, in The World Crisis, said that the story of the human race is war. Except for brief and precarious interludes, there has never been peace in our world.

What is Crisis Management? "The science and art of employing the political, economic, psychological and military forces of a nation or group of nations to afford the maximum support to adopted policies in peace or war." (Webster's New Collegiate Dictionary, 1994.)

The former east bloc represents one of the great challenges facing the west today. Its history is deep with tradition, unique in character, and replete with difficulties regarding the human aspects of crisis management.

The communist legacy of the former Eastern European Empire has had tremendous implications on the emerging "new Eastern Europe." How did it begin and why? Madeleine Albright, now U.S. Secretary of State, wrote in 1991 about the Communist legacy:

> "The Soviets established their Eastern European Empire for three reasons: First: For security, as a buffer zone to prevent future invasions from the west. Second: For economic benefits, to use the manufacturing capability of the satellites to support the Soviet Union. Third: For ideological purposes, to show that Marxism-Leninism was so attractive that it was being adopted by other countries. The combination produced short-term results and long-term problems as quite different countries were forced to mold their political and economic systems to fit the Soviet pattern. (Albright, 1991)

The Communists were molding more than political viewpoints and economies. There are long-term psychological problems that will take perhaps generations to overcome. Two of the most important aspects of personality that were critically affected, and in some cases, irreparably damaged were trust and initiative.

Since 1990 I have traveled and worked in Eastern Europe on a regular basis. There is a paradoxical feeling that goes with this part of the world. On the one hand, I have felt their great kindness and curiosity about life and opportunities in the West and, on the other, I have felt their distance and distrust.

Many Russians, for example, recall the good old days when the former Soviet Union wielded power and fought for a system in which they believed, to varying degrees. Some of the people gave me the feeling of an old elegant lamp that had once shown brightly, and gave light to others, but now sits dim-lit, gathering dust, out of fuel.

The faces of many of the people whom I met in the streets or market places showed their years of hard life and long struggle. On one occasion, while producing a documentary on the people and the government's strides toward democratization and perestroika, I had the opportunity to interview many of the people crossing Red Square. It was winter and 40° below zero, but the gusting winds did not stop these tough people from stopping to chat with a frozen California camera crew. They shared their hopes and fears about the changing face of the then Soviet Union. There uniformly were two attitudes, resolve and skepticism.

On subsequent trips, we saw that broken promises had turned optimism to disillusionment and, as I came to know some of the people on a deeper level, I asked more probing personal questions about habitual life in a failing system. They described their daily attempt at crisis management.

Most described basic attempts to get bread on the table and keep it there. The rift between the haves and have-nots grew as communism's social fabric began to fray. Yet there were still dinner invitations to modest meals with hard-working people.

I recall a conversation with a senior official from the Ministry of Finance. We were doing a documentary entitled Red Fall, so the camera was rolling.

I asked him, "How are you doing in your fight to turn the economy around?"

This was not exactly like asking someone about the death of his mother or the rape of his sister, but his face went crimson as though it had been. His response was controlled, prepared, and professional, as one would expect from a major player in a failing government. Something was wrong, however, in his non-verbal reaction so I asked the question again and this time my observational switch was on and I saw his non-verbal leak clearly. His eyes momentarily flashed shiny with tears and his jaw muscles instantly pulsed with fury.

"Why, are you so sad and angry?" I asked.

He was caught off guard by the directness of my question, and he answered immediately in English.

"My wife!" he said glaring at me.

The therapist in me came out, and a mundane interview of a bureaucrat turned into a conversation of some substance between two ordinary people.

"You see me sitting here in this warm office, talking of our grand plans to rescue our struggling economy, and my wife yesterday stood six hours in the freezing cold for a loaf of bread. It makes me angry and sad that I can do nothing about this now."

Crisis management is always personal because we, as people, are either victim of other's attempts to manage crisis or victims of our own efforts. When one thinks about it, in some ways, all of our lives reflect our personal and professional attempts at crisis management and, as one of my country western heroes, Jerry Jeff Walker, sings, "Some days are diamonds and some days are stone." In Russia, tourists visit the diamonds, and the people live with the stones. It will be so for a long time to come.

If distrust were a grain of sand, the people of the Eastern Bloc would be living in a desert. Corruption is systematic, deceit, a way of life, and doubt, a perpetual guest that shows in most every eye and handshake. These people have been victims of legions of lying leaders for decades. It wasn't only the communists who controlled their people with fear and falsehood; many others embraced these means of influence.

In May of 1996 Drs. Paul Meertz and I were invited to lead an international conference entitled Peace Building in the Caucasus. Attending the conference were representatives from Abkjazia, Armenia, Azerbaijan, Chechnya, Dagestan, Georgia, Ingushetia, Kabardino Balkarya, Krasnodarky Kray, Nagorky Karabakh, North Ossetia, Russia, South Ossetia, Stavropolsky Kray and Ukraine.

Over a four-day period increasingly important Chechnian leaders from that tumultuous region began to appear. On the last day in the evening Paul and I were asked to attend an urgent meeting in a nearby hotel room. Top parliamentary and judicial leaders came to discuss a key question. Also present at the meeting was a member of the Russian Douma. These leaders were considering a meeting with President Yeltsin to discuss the issues in the region. They considered this possibility with apprehension and distrust. They asked for our advice.

To many Russians, the Chechnians were criminals. The fact was that the majority of organized crime in Russia was controlled by the Chechnians. They had a real image and credibility problem. For the Chechnians, the Russians were little more than oppressors and terrorists.

The international concerns were that there was pressure from Moscow to stay linked to the old Soviet Union model. Corruption under the old Soviet Union became institutionalized organized crime when the collapse took place.

Some factors supported Chechnya in its resistance to Moscow. In fact, some Russian and Ukrainian officers were fighting with the Chechnians.

The same universal questions emerged once again in this international dispute. How do you overcome the pre-existing prejudices of those with whom you must negotiate?

President Yeltsin presents a non-verbal message, which reflects his two valued way of looking at life. There's the right way of doing things and then there is your way.

The Chechnians felt their sovereignty had been violated, and outrageous acts of terrorism had been perpetrated upon them. Both sides felt distrust and hostility toward one another. So it was that both sides saw themselves as the righteous, sitting across from criminals and terrorists. The question that we were asked was: If a meeting with the President were to take place, what would be the best way to approach President Yeltsin, given his prejudices and personality?

I suggested that five things had to be overcome by both sides:

- HINVL issues had to be let go. Historical conflicts and grievances about loss and injustice had to be put aside if genuine progress was to be made.

- Resistance to the natural tendency to fall back into the past had to be overcome. It is so easy to regress to earlier patterns of thinking in stressful situations.

- Both had to strive to be open to new and novel solutions as they were presented. Substantive change needed to be proceeded by substantive offers. All needed to be open to hear them when they were presented.

- A re-symbolization of past perceptual balance would be necessary. A rethinking of prices and payoffs would be necessary.

- Perhaps the most difficult issue was how to talk to a closed mind and keep yours open at the same time.

The end result of our meeting was that a face to face contact with President Yeltsin took place. This in itself was an important step in moving toward the resolution of conflict in the region. Following that initial meeting, other meetings took place. One took place in The Peace Palace in The Hague. This one was attended again by Drs. Paul Meertz* who had been present at the first meeting.

---

* Drs. Doctorandus, equivalent to a masters degree

This time the vice-president of Chechnya, the minister of foreign affairs and the President of the High Court were present. Representing the Russian side was Mr. Berezovski, a member of the national security counsel and one of the richest men in Russia with major holdings in Chechnya. Also present were members of the Russian Douma.

The meeting was chaired by the Presidents from Inguchetia and Tatarstand. The meeting was organized by the Americans, and the Chief mediator was Wm. Ury and Drs. Paul Meertz. The result was some progress in a continued effort to find a common ground. No breakthrough was reached, but another step was taken in an effort to find peace in the Caucasus.

What can be learned from this is that opportunities often spring from a desperate need to find harmony and balance within one's self and one's environment. What brought both sides to the negotiating table was perceived imbalance. In a certain way it stemmed from the HINVL. The perceived trauma was exacerbated over the years by failed communication, misperception and a reinforcement of perceived traumatic events. The past is a base for prejudice, and the present is the gift of now where change can take place. Efforts continue, but a beginning was found.

Of course, there are 27 different stories, one for each country that we in the west call Eastern Europe. In Lithuania, organized crime, although denied as a major influence by some government officials, has a major effect on the country's attempt to establish a free market economy and full democratization.

We were greeted with enthusiasm as we disembarked the plane to do a seminar on the human aspects of crisis management.

"Welcome to the wild, wild east," exhorted our host. It turned out that his greeting held more truth than humor. Some months earlier a journalist named Lingus, who wrote extensively about the Lithuanian Mafia for the Rispublika newspaper, was murdered in front of his home. The "Vilnius Brigade," as the local Mafia is called, was reputedly the executioner. The authorities arrested and held on murder charges, Boris Dekanidze, the son of the supposed Mafia Don, George Dekanidze.

One of the other objectives in our visit was to produce a television program in co-operation with Lithuanian National Television. My son Eric, who was our producer and director, and I were issued official press credentials. The murder case was Lithuania's O.J. Simpson trial, so I wanted to include it in the documentary. We made some inquiries between the formally scheduled interviews with cabinet members, President Brazauks and former President Landsburgas. Finally we got a telephone number. Mafia bosses are not listed in the phone directory under "M." I wanted information on the role of organized crime in Lithuania, so I thought, "Who better to interview than its reputed leader?"

An appointment was set and, camera crew and all, we arrived at the Vilnius Hotel. The foyer was filled with gray-suited gangsters with necks the size of garbage can lids. Al Capone would have fit right in. Sitting at the end of a long mahogany table was a squat man wearing a maroon suit. He extended his meaty hand and stubby fingers, exposing an old, faded anchor tattoo on his wrist. We had a government translator with us, and it was agreed that the interview was going to be conducted in Russian, not Lithuanian. Eric set up quickly and, as the lights went on, the Don and I began to talk via the translator.

Flanking Dekanidze were four associates, one clearly from the Middle East and another, whom I thought might be German. The other two I could not place. The time code on the videotape later revealed exactly five minutes had passed before I said to him, "I hear you are the head of the Mafia. Are you?"

The moment my cards were on the table, a smile came to his lips and then a hearty laugh. "How can I be? The Mafia is Italian and American; I'm Georgian and live in Lithuania!"

I fired back. "You know what I mean; Eastern European organized crime!"

He smiled a smile I'll never forget. For a moment the room went cold under the hot TV lights.

"I hear that about me," he said.

The scheduled fifteen-minute conversation lasted fifty. He wanted to get his story out to an American audience. At the end of the interview, he invited us to stay for lunch. I declined, as we had other interviews scheduled and I thought I had pushed my luck enough for the moment.

"Oh," he said ominously, "You won't eat with me?"

I explained our schedule to him.

"What about dinner at my house?"

Later we rode out of town 46 kilometers, in a bulletproof Mercedes, to a castle situated on one of Lithuania's many lakes. He had the 40-foot ceilings decorated with reproductions of Michelangelo's paintings on the Sixtine Chapel. The only difference was that the cherub's heads were portraits of his wife.

I interviewed Dekanidze another time. This time it was different; he was warm toward Eric and me. However, he was depressed because his son had been found guilty of conspiracy to murder and had been sentenced to death.

Their method is unique in fashion. It is a combination of the old, wild West and new, wild East. The prisoner remains in prison for up to a year, during which, at anytime, day or night, with only two hours notification, the executioner can enter the cell and shoot him in the back of the head! It was truly the wild, wild East.

The last time we were there, they where considering repealing the death penalty. For Dekanidze, it was bad timing. Boris Dekanidze was executed. His father claimed his body. Both the Don and his charming wife disappeared. The Vilnius Hotel was sold. Boris was later sighted on the streets of Vilnius, New York and Tel Aviv. He seems to have gotten around in death almost as much as Elvis.

I have heard that approximately 50% of the judges in Lithuania are on the take, and 50% the government officials are on the Mafia payroll. The Ministers of this emerging democracy earn approximately $150 per month. As a result of the training programs we conducted, our team was regularly in contact with all of the cabinet members and other officials. With few exceptions, I can say that these individuals were hard working, dedicated people who, as the expression says, "put their money where their mouths are," if you can say working 15 to18 hours a day, six days a week, for $150 a month, can be considered money.

The suggestion that these people were guilty of criminal activity is hard to believe and easy to rationalize due to the intolerable circumstances under which they live.

One of Lithuania's most popular and respected politicians was the former Prime Minister Adolfas Slezvicius. His desire to see new skills for his Government Ministers resulted in him ordering all of the Ministers to attend our training on the human aspects of crisis management. At a certain moment, the crisis management and organized crime portion of our program brushed a little close to the current realities. Some crooks somehow had electronically transferred millions from two of the largest banks. Reuter reported the story this way:

> "Lithuania aims to calm tensions over bank crashes. Vilnius, Jan.11, 1996. The government of the Baltic States of Lithuania, reeling from the shock closure of its top two banks, said on Thursday, it would start paying small bank depositors to ease tension among the population.

> "Prime Minister Adolfas Slezvicius also prepared to meet International Monetary Fund (IMF) and World Bank Officials after the central bank closed the Innovation and Litimpeks banks – the country's first and second largest – at the end of 1995. Slezevicius, under a cloud of scandal after it came out that he withdrew his personal savings from Innovation just two days before it was shut, promised that people with small deposits in the two banks would be the first to get their money back. Slezevicius will meet IMF and World Bank officials on Thursday. They will advise on whether the two banks should be salvaged and, if so, how. Slezevicius insisted that an election, ahead of the scheduled ballot in October, would not take place. "It would be of no use to have elections now. First we must solve the problems of the banking system," he said. (Lannin, 1996)

Later a reluctant President Brazausks was forced to ask for his resignation. It appeared that he had information that was too good at the wrong time. The Minister of Interior, who was instrumental in the prosecution of Boris Dekanidze, was also forced from office.

Gerrit "Jerry" F. de Gooyer, a police officer who worked for twenty-five years in municipalities, state and worldwide investigations, retired and took a position as Senior Vice President of ABN/AMRO bank. Periodically, Jerry joins our team as we travel to different East Bloc countries. In his current position, he is Director of the Corporate Security Department for his bank, which is the 16th largest in the world. He lectures on Eastern European organized crime, money laundering and bank fraud. On one trip he spoke to Lithuanian leaders and made, in part, these remarks:

> "Particular new private businesses are a target for organized crime. Almost all new companies are asked, in a short period after starting business, to pay some money to protectors. The Russian Ministry of Internal Affairs estimates that, in 1993, organized crime controlled approximately 40% of the total turnover in goods and services. They also say that approximately 5,700 organized crime groups were operating in Russia, seven times more than four years ago.

> "Organized crime has infiltrated banks, real estate markets and stock exchanges. Do not make the mistake that the word Mafia is used only to describe an organized criminal gang. In your language and society, the word Mafia is used for any criminal activity whereby a lot of money is involved. In the West, the word Mafia is connected with the Cosa Nostra organization in a hierarchical structure, as I mentioned earlier.

> "Now the question is why, in the East, is organized crime so eminent. For us, a number of reasons were found.

- No difference in wealth before the Glasnost. Therefore, now you see the differences and want, by any means, a piece of the pie.

- Differentiation in payment and status.

- Possibilities to make a fast big deal with a huge profit.

- Inadequate government repression system in laws as well in as in manpower, money, equipment and motivation.

- Corruption in all layers of the society. In the first quarter of 1994, 1909 police officers were charged with corruption in Moscow.

- Presence of easy targets, relatively rich foreigners.

- Drunkenness and drug use.

- Unemployment.

- Border obstacles diminished.

- Surplus of classified army goods.

- A great number of ex-police officers joining the organized crime groups as advisors."

"Almost all the laws are outdated and inadequate to tackle the present organized crimes. They are not up to date with the present technology. The government still considers wealth as being a capitalistic item and therefore something illegal. However it still considers a crime toward the state or state official far more serious than the same crime against a private citizen or company. So, if you steal from a person, you get milder punishment than if you steal from the government. It sounds reasonable as, formerly, the state was richer than the private persons were."

As in the West, in the East, banks and organized crime are an integral part of business. Nobody will say it, but considers it as a secret. In particular, the banks in Europe see vast amounts of money coming from the East through typical ML schemes and, when the security departments of those banks are investigating it, the ultimate source is mostly criminal money. Do not forget that, under the communist regime, those money channels already existed for the government. However, before funneling money to the West, one has to make a deposit. That is no problem, as only approximately 30 Russian banks are to be considered as recognizable banks, out of the 2000. So there are approximately 1970 banks at which you can deal about the possibilities to transfer any amount. The reasons for laundering the money can be various: From drug proceeds, laundering for buying hi-tech equipment, laundering for the purchase of the arms, precious metals, diamonds, radioactive material, clandestine removal of former communist's assets or funds and on and on.

However, if one faces any problem at any Russian or Lithuanian bank, he just takes a suitcase, puts the money in it, tips some official, crosses over the border, and off he goes. There are enough banks in the East which are already infiltrated by the Russian Mafia, so there is no need for going abroad."

Clearly, the people who live in the East Bloc, live in a situation of grave crisis on many levels. Few would dispute that crisis would be a word used to depict the plight of those living in these deplorable circumstances compared especially to those of us in the west.

Another factor that is standing in the way of their dealing with their crisis situation, is the manner in which they deal with women. There is a universal atmosphere of blatant sexism. I am not on Gloria Steinem's Christmas list, but what I saw on all levels of the society made me want to be. Just before the fall of the USSR, I was asked by the Soviet leadership, specifically the Council of Ministers, to do a training for them. They had heard about my work at the Clingendael Institute in The Hague.

The group was assembled in a fabulous birch-paneled room with the largest crystal chandelier I ever saw. I remember thinking that, if these fellows could get it down from that 50-foot ceiling, they could sell it, and their financial worries would be over! The room was arranged in the shape of a horseshoe. I was in the middle with my four assistants and a closed circuit television system.

I began the seminar by showing the participants their NVLs. The fifth or sixth person to come in front of the video was a man who looked like former Chairman Brezhnev. He wore a cheap Russian suit and a golden smile. I asked him to say the name of someone important to him. He said, "My wife, Natasha."

I had him repeat it three times. We do this to make sure that the NVL response is not an accident or the result of some other non-related factors. Each time he said her name, he closed his eyes, put his tongue out, and swallowed down. I asked him to say the way that he used to call his mother when he was a child. He obliged me and once again he gave the same non-verbal leak. He spoke only Russian, but this was no problem as the entire program was being translated simultaneously. I asked him to take off his earpiece for a moment. When he did, I explained to his comrades that he clearly had problems with women. Those problems came from an unresolved traumatic event(s), which originated with his mother (PTE). Because it was an NVL and not a random response, I was confident that it would repeat again. He will close his eyes etc., etc.

"Put in your ear-piece again," I said. His NVL was just as I had forecast.

When I suggested that he had difficulties with women and that he did not trust them, he laughed and said, "Don't we all!"

After the roaring sexist laughter died down, I asked him a question.

"Minister, how many women work in your Ministry?"

"I do not know, tens of thousands, I guess."

"Do you admit having difficulty trusting and relating to women?"

"So what? All men do," he said, beginning to grimace.

"Let me ask you one more question, if I might. Do you really want to help your country in this time of major economic crisis?"

"Of course!" he bellowed in Russian. The look said it all. It was translated anyway. The ice seemed to be getting thin as the room began to become silent.

"Minister," I said, realizing that the Gulag was much closer than sunny California, "you are not using a great resource as well as you could. I am talking about the women in your ministry." I went on. The room was absolutely silent now.

"You need to work on this problem if you are really serious."

He thanked me with a golden smile. We had a very nice conversation later. It is no wonder that motivation is wanting in much of the population considering the lack of genuine respect given those who are not in positions of power. This is foolish and will add years to their social and economic recovery from what Madeleine Albright called the Communist legacy of the former Eastern European Empire.

NATO, of course, has a great interest in the development and stability of Russia, Ukraine, and the Partnership for Peace (PFP) countries, as well as the would-be PFP countries. Democratic principles are simply principles of communication, interaction and appropriate responses.

To enter into full membership of the European family, these principles will have to be practically translated into realistic means of managing the human aspects of crisis management effectively. This naturally means all of its citizenry.

When an individual stands in judgment of another's worth, the effect is to limit and distort the communication process and perhaps delimit freedom of expression. When this occurs on the short term, there is resistance upon the part of those whose views are not heard or respected. When this persists on the long-term, systems begin to break down. On the individual level, psychopathology may develop, and therapy may become necessary. When communication breaks down at the national level, human rights are neglected, and racism, sexism, and feelings of judgment may lead to conflict and violence.

When this phenomenon occurs on an international level, a governmental collapse is only a matter of time, as we saw in the former Soviet Union. Unequivocal deferential communication is the underlying principle to any democracy and the true key to lasting crisis management. Crisis management skills relate directly to communication skills. Moreover, communication is most effective when there is mutual consideration of differences in cultural values and style. This fact is reflected in these bipartisan remarks which are ultimately sound concepts of communication and crisis management.

John F. Kennedy said, on January 11,1962, in his State of the Union Address, "Yet our basic goal remains the same: a peaceful world community of free and independent states, free to choose their own future and their own system, so long as it does not threaten the freedom of others."

Ronald Reagan, two decades later, on June 8, 1982 said, in his Address to the British Parliament, "For the sake of peace and justice, let us move toward a world in which all people are at least free to determine their own destiny."

The largest and most effective Crisis Management organization in the world ever is the North Atlantic Treaty Organization. With the assistance and might of the United States, communism was defeated. Now there are other challenges facing this grand alliance that test its commitment to peace in Europe.

People now taking their first breath of freedom in seventy plus years, as is the case in Yugoslavia, seem to have learned little and remembered much. Years of oppression seem to have done little to erase the memories of old perceived injuries as the struggle of Serbian irregulars in Croatia or Bosnia and Herzegovina attest.

European crisis management has rapidly and systematically evolved since the collapse of the Warsaw Pact. Many of the problems of European security have been re-evaluated in light of the massive shift of the geopolitical relationships between East and West. As recently as 1991, there were many questions about NATO's role and value in European security. David Robertson, in an article about NATO's future, wrote:

"Even if NATO is the last and best hope, there are formidable problems, and no guarantee it can solve them. The problems can be broken into three aspects: Who are the members? What is the political justification? What is the operational doctrine and force structure?"

"The membership question follows from the change of role. NATO cannot continue to be a defense of Western Europe against Eastern Europe or the WTO. There no longer is an eastern bloc, and the WTO has collapsed. If Europe needs a stabilizing security arrangement, these unstable Eastern European states must be involved.

Unless something is done about this identity problem, NATO could at best be a rival security organization."

(Robertson, 1991)

I decided to gather more information on NATO's direction into the next millennium, so recently, I spoke with Leo Verbruggen, the Executive Secretary of NATO, and he was kind enough to write down what he feels NATO's short and long-term concerns will be. Here are what are seen as the challenges that are likely to remain on NATO's transatlantic agenda well into the next century.

- In principle, to resist the political winds that shift, blow and alter the directions of NATO's ship of state.

- To insure growth, vitality and consistency while keeping the operational outlook on a clear course.

- To help shape, develop and assist in the building of a viable European security and defense framework.

- To keep the transatlantic security framework healthy and reconciled with European integration.

- To fairly balance NATO's burden between allies on both sides of the Atlantic.

- To establish a lasting strategic partnership with Russia and Ukraine while maintaining a continued close relationship with partners.

- To reach out to the Mediterranean neighboring countries.

- To create with partners, new and even more effective means for the prevention and management of crisis.

Many Americans are ignorant of what NATO is and what role it has played in maintaining peace and keeping the Communists and Warsaw Pact in check. Perhaps this is due to a combination of three things:

- American chauvinism.

- Media's general neglect of the world that exists beyond America's shores.

- Questionable priorities such as a greater interest in important things like trapped whales, babies who have fallen into wells, and President Clinton's sex life.

The good news and the bad news, with regard to American chauvinism, is the same: we believe in ourselves. The economy is booming, the stock market soaring, and inflation is low. The U.S. is not involved in any hot war, and the old cold war has cooled to the point that it is more history than news. It's backyard barbecues, family life and people enjoying the American dream or struggling to keep it from becoming an American nightmare. Epictetus, almost two thousand years ago, asked, "Is freedom anything but the right to live as we want? Nothing else."

Mort Rosenblum, an old pal and special correspondent for the Associated Press, and former Editor-in-Chief of the International Herald Tribune, wrote a book about the media's neglect. It spelled out the media's methods for selling itself in America.

In *Who Stole the News?* he explains why the American public has become deaf to NATO's message:

"Correspondents are better equipped now than they have ever been, steeped in background, driven to excel and supported by technology only dreamed about a decade ago. And yet few Americans are able to follow distant events, which shape their lives. Most are shown generalities, simplicities and vast empty spaces, a parody of the real world beyond their borders."

"Many news executives believe that Americans do not really care about themselves. Their organizations scrimp on the space they devote to serious news, favoring impact over information and neglecting the subtle but vital undercurrents. They slash away at the corners, gambling that no one will notice. In doing this, they reinforce the ignorance they assume."

"The goal of news executives is to increase their ratings or circulation and to enhance their organizations" standings. If convinced that people wanted better coverage of the world, they would hurry to provide it. Surveys suggest that the demand is out there. If so, people had better speak up. This is easier than you think."   (Rosenblum, 1993)

Reporter Arthur Kent in his book, Risk and Redemption, said: "Not only is the fluff index growing, but news reporting agencies like NBC are giving foreign news reporting two-thirds less coverage than ten years earlier."

We prioritize our lives. How often do you call your parents or do your kids call you to check in? We, as people in general, forget the important relationships unless it is a holiday or there is an emergency. There is no emergency in Europe, at least in the American perception as I have seen it. There is passing interest in Croatia or Bosnia and Herzegovina, and this usually relates to media reporting about U.S. troop involvement, flare-ups or length of commitment to the region. Christmas seems a ways off.

These are the times that are, in a way, most difficult for individuals and groups that are charged with keeping the peace. It could be argued that we are so busy enjoying the peace that we risk losing it to a constant enemy of freedom: complacency. While many Americans are ignorant and complacent of the benefits or even existence of NATO, other countries scramble to get under its productive umbrella.

On July 8, 1997, the NATO Ministerial meetings took place in Maria. The expansion of NATO was one of the issues discussed.

A decision was taken to begin the initial negotiations with three countries, which would eventually lead to full membership in NATO around the year 2000. Later, in the Hungarian parliament, the issue of membership was voted upon. Before the unanimous vote of 217 was taken, a spirited discussion took place. Some of the remarks made during the debate illustrated the merits of this crisis management organization.

"NATO is not needed because we are in a dangerous situation now, but in order that this unthreatening period would continue to remain stable for a long time to come."

With regard to the impact to the economy, he remarked that, "Asking the price of membership in NATO is like posing the question before the flood, What would it cost to purchase a ticket on Noah's ark?" (Ivan Szabo, MDNP party leader)

The final political resolution and declaration said, in part:

> "The summit was a milestone in NATO's role in the formation of a new European security system. The summit decision to expand the alliance is a historically significant one. This opens up a new chapter in the relations of NATO with the East Central European region, supports the regions Democratic Development, strengthens the stability and security of Europe, and promotes the creation of unity of the continent. It puts an end for good to Europe's cold war heritage."

Prime Minister Horn Gyula put it plainly: "Our country and nation are at stake. Selling NATO or the expansion of NATO is difficult in a lazy Sunday afternoon."

The remarks of H.F. Byrd belong in the headline in America's Sunday newspaper. "Freedom is an achievement of men, and as it was gained by vigilance and struggle, it can be lost by indifference and suppleness." All men and women need to remember this remark.

The attempts to find a peaceful settlement to the difficulties facing the Middle East seem bogged down because of two fundamental issues, the HINVL and the inability to be open to difference.

When one generation teaches another to distrust or hate another person or group, the self-fulfilling prophecy will work its will. The Historical Interactive Non-Verbal Leak (HINVL) serves as a generation guide to seeing and evaluating the events that we experience on a daily basis.

The poisoned cup spills over from one generation to another to the extent that the individual from the previous generation has failed to work through two issues: one, being open to differences in others and two, seeing violence as a justifiable approach to problem solving.

It is a paradox to me that all three of the major religions in the region profess love, understanding and acceptance of all others regardless of their belief systems. Yet the body count grows and grows. Love thy neighbor remains more wish than fact.

As long as all sides of the struggle make judgments about loyalty to the cause of individuals who call for negotiations and talks, there will be reluctance to join in and enforce the peace process. One of my major mentors, Dr. Bill Pemberton says this about the situation:

'Probably one of the most insidious of the dangerous doctrines is the doctrine of exclusivity, that only our prophet has the correct translation/interpretation of the cosmos. American poet Carl Sandburg said, that "exclusive" is the worst word in the English language. The word "exclusive" makes some feel superior to others and frequently builds distance and often distrust. The feeling, if not the word, has found its way to the Middle East. The word and idea of crisis and crisis management will also be in the future for a long time, too." (Pemberton, 1989)

Pemberton makes another point about how religions that preach love and acceptance can end up mistranslated by some of their followers:

"An example in the sphere of religion: Historically, at a given time, a major prophet has appeared on planet Earth. His followers have written down the wisdom, ratified it, deified it, and then made it into an exclusivity doctrine, "Only our prophet has the truth!"
(from a deity).

"A neuro-semantic approach gives us a quantum leap out of this paradox. One of the truisms of being human is that similarities or commonalties unite us, and differences or uniqueness sometimes alienate us."
(Pemberton, 1989)

Lasting peace in the region has a real chance when all peoples are treated with respect and equality under the law. Inequality fosters resentment, resentment breeds hostility, and hostility leads to the rationalized expression of violence. Violence is a communication about a lack of communication. To achieve effective communication, all people must strive to overcome their personal biases and past negative experiences.

Some of the worlds' great thinkers and philosophers are from that part of the world. These ideas are not new; it is just a matter of blending the insight with the right actions and learning how to get along with the others in the sandbox. I remain sanguine but not overly optimistic. When the Gulf war broke out, I did an analysis of Saddam Hussein for some European governmental officials and NATO authorities who were taking a course I was offering at the Clingendael Institute in the Hague. Later, in Moscow, I gave the same course for the Council of Ministers and repeated the same analysis. Without going into sensitive material, I can say without doubt that this leader is as ruthless as his detractors suggest. There is an old Indian expression that I shared with the participants, "If you are going to kill a snake, kill it while it is young." I am not advocating assassination, simply snake removal.

I am a great believer in crisis management techniques and communication as being possible with most all people, but I do not kid myself that we can reach all individuals. There is a snake growing in the gulf that is now six years

too old, and it is only a matter of time until it strikes again.
You can bet your NVL on that. The same principles that
govern child-rearing behavior apply to the world affairs
consideration. When one accepts the unacceptable, he
reinforces it.

The political ping-pong game played by Saddam Hussein
and the United Nations and their inspectors will ultimately
fail to reach a peaceful resolution. The reason that the
United Nations coalition, which previously fought in Iraq,
or a bilateral force of US and British forces, will have to
enter the Gulf is, because Saddam's definition of peace is
incompatible with basic human rights. It is only a matter
of time that what should have been done will have to be
done. President Clinton and Prime Minister Tony Blair
have both announced the necessity of establishing a new
and more just regime in Iraq.

Reading the non-verbal leak of Saddam Hussein* could
lead one to the conclusion that his definition of reality and
appropriate behavior will assure only additional pain and
suffering in the region. Here is an example where insight
without action will again lead to anxiety and action without
insight will lead to additional chaos.

Three top experts, familiar with the situation, offered a
current observation about foreign policy concerns in the
region.

> "Every president since Richard Nixon has recognized
> that ensuring Persian Gulf security and stability is a
> vital U.S. interest."

> "The Clinton administration's strategy for achieving
> this goal during the president's first team was its
> attempted dual containment of Iraq and Iran. This is
> more a slogan than a strategy, however, and the policy
> may not be sustainable for much longer. In trying to
> isolate both of the Gulf's regional powers, the policy
> lacks strategic viability and carries a high financial
> and diplomatic cost. Saddam Hussein is still in power
> six years after his defeat at the hands of a

---

* It is not appropriate to include this information here

multinational coalition, and the international consensus on continuing the containment of Iraq is fraying. The strident U.S. campaign to isolate Iran, in turn, drives Iran and Russia together, and the United States and its Group of Seven allies apart."

"Finally, the imposing U.S. military presence that helps protect members of the Gulf Cooperation Council (GCC) from external threats is being exploited by hostile elements to take advantage of internal social, political, and economic problems."

"The advent of the Clinton's administration's second term, together with the imminent inauguration of a new administration in Iran following this May's election, provides an opportunity to review U.S. policies toward the Gulf and consider whether midcourse correction could improve the situation."

(Brzezinski et al, 1997)

"Ethnic conflict is keeping Africa from sharing in the worlds' prosperity." (Deutch, 1997)

Africa will never be the great continent it could be until and unless its leaders climb out of the sandbox and help their people to follow.

Tribalism is like many other "isms," racism, sexism, anti-Semitism, and all the rest because all are based upon the same foolish notion, an individual or group thinking that they are better than someone else. Rouhana Nadim N. & Bar-Tal D. commented, in an article titled Psychological Dynamics of Intractable Ethnonational Conflicts, that:

"Conflicts between and among states that dominated the international scene for decades are gradually being replaced by conflicts between ethnic, religious, linguistic, and national groups within the states, often termed ethnonational conflicts"

(Connor, 1994).

"The conflicts between Catholics and Protestants in Northern Ireland, Tamils and Hindus in Sri Lanka, Muslims and Serbs in Bosnia, and Tutsi and Hutu in Rwanda are only a few examples of ethnonational conflicts raging around the world. Dealing with these conflicts introduces new challenges to the international system because of the ostensible intractability of the conflicts; the underestimation of the psychological dynamics that can contribute to their escalation, stalemate, and perpetuation." (Rubin, Pruitt, & Kim, 1994); and the difficulty of applying traditional efforts to their resolution (Rouhana, 1998). These conflicts, also termed deep-rooted (Burton, 1987), enduring rivalry (Goertz & Diehl, 1993), or protracted social conflicts (Azar, 1990), are often transformed into intractable social conflicts (Kriesberg, 1993) that defy traditional negotiation and dedicated efforts." (Azare, 1990; Burton, 1990) It is obvious, by the aforementioned remarks, that new tools are necessary to resolve these worldwide growing conflicts. The reading of the non-verbal leak can surface the heretofore untapped hostilities and differences in perception. Once surfaced to a conscious level of awareness, a deeper discussion about perceived wrongs may result in a more fruitful outcome than we have achieved in the past. Ultimately, it will boil down to people forgiving other people for being human and not perfect in the way they relate to each other. Fancy philosophies, beliefs, or long histories of tradition do not make this strategy any more valid. Perhaps this self-destructive narcissism plays a key role in most of our personal or foreign policy disputes.

The other key factor is a perceived insult on the part of one group by another. Another consideration is the position of power one group has over another. Circumstances are always changing and therefore, degrees of influence and spheres of influence are always shifting. Winston Churchill pointed up this fact when he said: "Time is a changeable ally." (Broadcast, March 30,1940)

Years of doing the same old dumb thing does not make it smart. The concept of the HINVL may offer some explanation of this behavior. Consider this story from when I was working in Africa in the Ivory Coast.

The CEO of a major company representing all African Nations made an appointment for an NVL screening. He was to receive feedback about himself, and evaluate the system for possible use within his company.

I waited in my office for this VIP to arrive. After 25 minutes passed, I began to wonder whether there was some confusion about the time. It was right there in my agenda: 11 a.m. A few minutes later a limousine drove up and in walked a tall-distinguished looking man. He made no excuses. Extending his hand he said, "Where do I sit?"

"In the chair facing the front of the monitor," I said. "You are almost 40 minutes late."

"Yes, what do we do now? Do I look at you or myself in the monitor?"

"Okay, Sir. You want to be like that," I thought. "Face the monitor and say your name."

He did and, at the same time, he closed his eyes and swallowed down. Each time I asked him to do it again, the same thing happened.

"Look, you came here late. I assume that is because you are a very busy man so, why don't you say your real name?"

When I finished my remark, he was still sitting in the chair, barely. Needless to say he did not appreciate some yank coming 9,000 miles to his country to call him a liar. Through his clenched teeth he looked at me with a look that made me realize why he was the BIG boss.

"That is my name," he said in a low, flat voice almost as well as Clint Eastwood might have said it. I waited for him to add the word, "Punk." He didn't. We continued.

"Come on. Say your real name," I pressed.

"Okay," he said and he repeated what to my ears sounded exactly, I mean exactly the same. That was the unconscious self-concept at work.

"Again, again!"

He appeased me and complied.

"I never say it that way because that is the way we pronounce it in my tribal village. I am from the Baule tribe, and the main population I work with here is Senufo so I use their pronunciation."

"Well, there it is; you have been swallowing your anger down for years and, moreover, you have been denying your identity to fit in with the main population."

This powerful man was in fact a little boy playing a game in someone else's multi-national sandbox, and he was angry.

Our bond was set there and then. The rest of the session was devoted to giving him more feedback about the process, but there was nothing that could top that true story of the man with two names.

A look at the basic issues facing Africa reveals the age-old struggle for survival and the terrific disparity between the haves and the have-nots. Mort Rosenblum wrote books that addressed some of the inequities in Africa, *Mission to Civilize the French Way* and *Squandering Eden: Africa at the Edge*, with Doug Williamson.

Mort writes about something that has to be seen to be appreciated. It is at the heart of what will give Africa, in general and the Ivory Coast in particular, a potential ingredient for unrest and crisis.

> "Up a four-lane superhighway in Yamoussoukro, a futuristic rural capital of grand esplanades, blazing lights, luxurious hotels, a sumptuous presidential palace, and hardly any visitors at all. Most nights, six lane freeways and elaborate cloverleafs serve only the occasional bicycle. Yamoussoukro is, coincidentally, the late Houphouet-Boigny's home village, and the president's flights of fancy raise eyebrows, if not hackles. Hard-pressed in the 1980's and with one of Africa's highest per-capita debts, he pushed ahead with lavish construction projects. In Abidjan, he built a huge cathedral, and then, as bankers negotiated a rescue package to reschedule the towering debt, he announced plans for a basilica at Yamoussoukro. Its dome would dwarf that of St. Peter's in Rome. Its cost, not announced, was expected to run into hundreds of millions of dollars."   (Rosenblum)

As long as this mentality endures, in business or in government, there will exist the basis for unrest and uproar. It is foolish to expect people to live in harmony with such inequities. The foundation for authentic crisis management within a society lays in laws that guarantee equal opportunity; but those laws must be supported by leaders who have the courage, power and resolve to see them applied on all levels of society.

"Commentaries on recent political developments in the sub-Saharan region run the gamut from giddy Afrophilia to gloomy Afropessimism. Early assessments were hopeful, seeing the peaceful electoral displacement of authoritarian regimes in countries like Benin and Zambia as harbingers of "political renewal" and a "second liberation."

(October 1992): 11-25; Dag Hammarskjold Foundation, *The State in Crisis in Africa: In Search of a Second Liberation* (Uppsala, Sweden: Dag Hammarskjold Foundation, 1992); and Gorran Hyden and Hyden Michael Richard Joseph, *Africa: The Rebirth of Political Freedom, Journal of Democracy.*

"A critical backlash soon followed in the wake of a series of disputed elections in places like Angola and Kenya. At best, analysts pondered thoughtfully about the sustainability of multiparty competition under conditions of ethnic fragmentation and elite corruption." (Rratton, 1992)

"At worst, they lapsed into apocalyptic warnings of impending civil disorder in the wake of the 'stalling winds of change'." (Lemarchand, 1993) The editors of Africa Demos (Atlanta, Georgia: The Carter Center) considered that "as the New Year (1993) begins, we are no longer so optimistic. The Struggle for democracy has been forced onto a new and disadvantageous plane." (February 1993): 14.

Africa's sandbox is full of many natural resources and, in that sense, there are potential riches. Whether they will be realized or remain lost to the people will determine the degree of crisis Africa will face.

On February 2, 1917, in a speech before the House of Commons, Churchill said, "Consideration for the lives of others and the laws of humanity, even when one is struggling for one's life and in the greatest stress, does not go wholly unrewarded." The Marquis of Queensbury rules of 1917 somehow failed to survive the journey from one end of the century to the other. Fractured bodies and buildings echo the cry of injustice of both the victims and victimizers. Media's great eyes and ears on a shrinking globe gives a front row seat that bring pain and plights up close and personal.

As the clichè says, "One person's patriot is another person's terrorist." Here again context determines meaning and perception determines reality. Terrorism results from a group's feeling that its views, values or needs are not being met, and more drastic measures are necessary and justified. It would appear that this issue would become more of a problem for the U.S.A. John Deutch, the former CIA Director, indicated that,

> "Pax Americana is going to result in more terrorism in
> and against American assets."   (Deutch, 1997)

All terrorists had mothers, fathers, and families. All terrorists are passionate people. All terrorism is a communication about a lack of communication. All terrorism is the nightmare of organized governments, a knife that rips at the fabric of democracy and, therefore, all crisis management efforts must be maximized to defeat their efforts. As I stated earlier, crisis management is a challenge for us all regardless of our stations in life or our professions. Our success in international crisis management ultimately depends on the art of diplomacy, which as someone said, is the art of being able to say "nice doggie" until you can pick up a rock. Our success will also depend on skills in the human aspects of crisis management.

19 CLINICAL PROFILE OF PRESIDENT SLOBODAN MILOSEVIC: OLD DECISIONS – NEW PAIN

The following lecture was presented at the beginning of NATO's air involvement. It was seen and read at NATO Headquarters.

THE ROLE OF THE UNCONSCIOUS IN MANAGEMENT CRISIS: PRESIDENT SLOBODAN MILOSEVIC AND THE KOSOVO CONFLICT

Professor Barry Austin Goodfield, PhD,
Director, The Goodfield Foundation for the Study of
Conflict, Communication and Peace Building,
Director, Goodfield Television Productions
May 10 1999

On March 31st of this year, in my capacity as visiting Professor at the Diplomatic Academy of London, I had the opportunity to present my views, which I again share in this paper, regarding President Slobodan Milosevic. I also presented them in an analysis of Milosevic on Tuesday March 30, 1999 on the BBC WORLD Television. It is my hope that the following observations will provide the basis for a deeper understanding of this individual who is causing so much death and destruction in Europe today.

"Smart bombs rain surgical destruction in Europe as old unconscious issues dictate to closed minds." This is a headline that could banner today's papers. Just how does old thinking govern today's conflicts?

This may be the first war started, which has to do with human rights violations. Is the human condition becoming more important as we approach a new millennium? How do our leaders' conscious and unconscious behaviors affect international crises and foreign affairs? A number of factors can be deduced about an individual's decisions and strategies by analyzing the non-verbal leaks that he presents.

FIVE ASPECTS GOVERNING THE UNCONSCIOUS SELF-CONCEPT

- Level of unresolved perceived traumatic events coming from, intrapsychic, psychophysiological, interpersonal, national or international factors.
- Evolvement of other traumas that reinforce the original trauma.
- Amount of incongruence between the conscious and unconscious self-concept.
- Knowledge which gives positive reinforcement of the conscious self-concept increases pressure on the unconscious self-concept.
- Severe pathology may develop when there is too much pressure resulting in a breakdown of the system.

CONSIDERATION OF THE CURRENT CRISIS IN KOSOVO

(What we know about human behavior in crisis is that with stress goes regression.)

- NATO forces attack Serbian targets in Yugoslavia with heavy bombing raids and cruise missiles in Belgrade and other areas.
- NATO reports that the initial strikes have been "successful".
- President Milosevic is being "taught" not to doubt NATO's resolve.
- Revenge attacks by Serb troops are under way.
- Ethnic Serbs and Kosovo Albanians cower in their homes.
- NATO's unity is holding for the moment.

BACKGROUND INFORMATION ON SLOBODAN MILOSEVIC

He had a traumatic background as a child including the suicide of both parents. He suffered depression, isolation and aloneness as a result of the war. As former head of the Communist party and later

He is married and has two children, a daughter Marija
and a son, Marko. His wife, Mirjana Markovic, Ph.D.,
is a tenured professor at the University of Belgrade
and a member of the Russian Academy of Social
Sciences.

Before entering politics, Mr. Milosevic had an
extensive career in management and banking. For
many years he was the President and CEO of
Tehnogas in Belgrade, one of the largest industrial
companies in Serbia. Subsequently he was the
President and CEO of Beobanka, the largest bank in
Yugoslavia at a time.

After entering politics, Mr. Milosevic held some of the
most important political appointments and elected
offices in the City of Belgrade and Republic of Serbia.
He is the founder and the President of the Socialist
Party of Serbia.

In 1990, in the first democratic elections in Yugoslavia
since World War II, Mr. Milosevic was elected President
of Serbia by a landslide. In the 1992 General
Elections, Mr. Milosevic was again elected President of
Serbia by an overwhelming majority of voters."

Web Site Federal Republic of Yugoslavia, May 5, 1999

As previously stated, Milosevic has surrounded himself
with people who reinforce his perceptions of reality. His
strongest supporter and some would even say his greatest
influence, is his wife Mirjana Markovic, Ph.D. She is an
important variable to consider when analyzing the Kosovo
conflict. Both Milosevic and his wife were orphaned early,
and they bonded together early. Milosevic has allied
himself with his wife's communist party to form a leftist
coalition that openly advocates the return of communist
rule to Yugoslavia.

The early contact born in crisis and tempered in turmoil
has made Milosevic's wife more than just his life's
companion. A two against the world grand alliance has laid
not just the practical base but the emotional base for his

fight and struggle in Yugoslavia. It is a Yugoslavian Mom and Pop store serving the people who fit his dictatorial view of democracy. They acted as surrogate parents for one another, trusting and confiding only in one another. This symbiotic relationship will delimit the amount of external feedback, which will be given serious consideration. He has surely surrounded himself with "true believers," people who are fanatically convinced of the correctness of his position. If President Milosevic were to be removed it would leave only a more determined and dogmatic widow surrounded by followers bent on avenging their martyred president.

If the toppling of Milosevic's government is to be considered, it will be necessary to remove as many individuals in his inner circle as possible one way or the other.

Those who are seen as not fitting into his two-valued logic (right-wrong, good-bad, like me-not like me) are seen as being against him, ill informed or not belonging to his dream for Yugoslavia. President Milosevic not only limits and controls the input that he gets about his behavior. His actions are those of a clever tactician behind the scenes. Like many charismatic leaders, he is charming, persuasive and clear about his worldview.

Borislav Jovic was president of Yugoslavia until just before the outbreak of the conflict in 1991, with battles between the former Yugoslav republics of Serbia and Croatia. He describes Milosevic as a leader who delights in court intrigue but makes all the decisions himself. He reports conversations in which Milosevic insists there will be a war by Serbia against the other republics of Yugoslavia, and says that as early as 1989 Milosevic had to be dissuaded from ordering the army to intervene in Slovenia. To pursue the Bosnian Serb rebellion against the Muslim-dominated government of Bosnia in 1992, Jovic writes, he and Milosevic devised the scheme of withdrawing from Bosnia all Yugoslav soldiers who were not Bosnian Serbs and replacing them with Bosnian Serbs who had been stationed in Serbia. In this way, he writes, about 90,000 Serbian soldiers remained in Bosnia and could be commanded by the local Serb leadership in the effort to create a greater Serbia.

A prima facie case for the indictment of Slobodan Milosevic Paul Williams and Norman Cigar – Balkan Institute.

NATO stands at the crossroads. If his actions are proven to be as atrocious as they are alleged to be, then it puts NATO's nineteen members in the position of choosing to negotiate with an alleged war criminal equaled only by the likes of Stalin or Hitler in this century. The dilemma is to remove him and his cronies by legal or military means and establish a new government or face the problem of negotiations with a war criminal.

It seems to me that the path that NATO has chosen must be followed to its logical conclusion. At the same time NATO must step up its willingness to negotiate if in fact they are willing to deal with Milosevic's government. If not, NATO must publicize clearly and repeatedly the inhumanity, death and destruction that resulted from his government. If negotiations is the path that is chosen, then Milosevic must be allowed to see himself as somehow victorious against NATO just as Sadam Hussein presented himself as victorious over President Bush's coalition.

The Kosovo Conflict provides a look into the thinking of President Milosevic. He clearly and rightly recognizes the necessity of waging war on two fronts.

One is the military confrontation with NATO and two is the media war where he fights for minds and not territory. He recognizes the importance of winning the war of words as this provides the ultimate base from which he will negotiate the conclusion of the conflict.

In a recent interview Milosévic made the following remarks:

> "The problem is the following. Your government (the United States) is running two wars against Yugoslavia, against our people. One is military war and the other war is media war or, if you like it better, propaganda war. Propaganda war started long before military war and its goal was to (demonize) this country, our people, leadership of this country, individuals, and

whatever was needed to create, artificially of course, public opinion in United States which will be supportive to aggression they committed later.

And uh, that media war is showing clearly that their intention to commit aggression for having the long preparation before. So, we are victims of both of those wars. In first case, in military war, victims are just for now our civilians and our country everywhere but in media war, victims are not only us. Victim is as well American democracy. If you're lying your citizens and if you're continually trying to create artificial public opinion based on, uh, false informations, on wrong informations you cannot call it democratic. You cannot tell to the world that you are doing something fair and fine. So I believe that, uh, this kind of contacts and more than that the presence of a lot of journalists from abroad in this country will help to the world to know the truth about our country."

Here again we see President Milosevic focusing on how he is a victim and how his people are victims. The natural course of action is to fight against the victimizers. His behavior is rationalized and the struggle legitimized. In his view it is only just and fair to fight against the overwhelming odds which he faces. So the more he sees himself as a victim, the easier it is to justify and rationalize the extreme behavior necessary for survival. What is interesting here is the cognitive dissonance, that is the denial of his own behavior and that of those around him.

Milosevic controls the media; it is in that sense an extension of the propaganda war, which he carefully runs from Belgrade. When "journalists" appear on television wearing targets on their lapels symbolizing their defiance to NATO's bombing, one must question their objectivity and journalistic distance. As stated earlier, Milosevic has created a closed system, which reinforces his own internal perceptions, which constitutes his reality. He accuses the United States and NATO of perverting the democratic process while he involves himself in ethnic cleansing and genocide with those whom he sees as unfit, unacceptable and unnecessary. This ability to rationalize information, which is inconsistent with his view of reality, is reflective of his capacity to isolate ideas and information, which are inconsistent with his views.

In a later part of the interview with Milosevic, Dr. Hatchett asks him about his background. He makes reference to the fact that he used to have friends in the United States and was familiar with the country. Now, of course, he is in conflict with the government of the U.S. and NATO.

> Dr. Hatchett: I think the American people would like to know a little bit more about you as a person though. Have you always been a politician; have you always been in politics?

> President Milosevic: Oh no, I was not politician. I professionally – I was professionally working in industry for a long time and then I was banker – for eight years. I was President of largest Yugoslav bank. At that time we were dealing with a lot of American banks and I had a lot of friends in the United States from that time.

This reinforces the earlier old decisions, namely: that trusting people and letting them get close only results in disappointment. People are not to be trusted. Distrust, deceit and denial are the fundamental core of Milosevic's personality.

His need for control and his willingness to do anything to sustain his position of power are reflected in the remarks of Associated Press writer, Jovana Gec:

> "Milosevic has dominated Serbia since rising to power in its then-ruling communist party in 1987. He won the first open elections in 1990 and again in 1992. Both times the opposition cried fraud; both times, Milosevic and his ruling Socialists denied the charges and prevailed. This time, the previously weak and splintered democratic opposition stands a better chance because it has united in a four-party alliance and is riding a wave of popular discontent. In Serbia,

which dominates its Yugoslav federation with Montenegro, people are fed up with a ruinous state-run economy, funding Serb rebellions in Croatia and Bosnia and the crippling international sanctions that ensued. Half the population is unemployed. Inflation is 100% per year.

"The sister party of Milosevic's Socialists in Montenegro is running against an opposition campaigning for greater independence from Serbia's overbearing embrace. Nevertheless, Milosevic hopes, with help from a tightly controlled media campaign, to maintain control over the 138-seat federal Yugoslav parliament."

"Current Yugoslav president Zoran Lilic was handpicked by Milosevic, who would need the support of the parliament to change the federal constitution to make the post important. The opposition alleges Milosevic will stop at nothing, including vote rigging, to win."

Jovana Gec, Associated Press Writer.
Oct. 30, 1996 BELGRADE, Yugoslavia (AP)

Milosevic has a winning strategy so far that may seem to some like the willingness to negotiate, but a closer look reveals what I call a yes-but strategy. Yes-but means no. At times he has presented a conciliatory image which on closer scrutiny reflected stalling tactics as he manipulated events and individuals behind the scenes.

Milosevic is probably not even consciously aware of his actions, as they have become such a habitual pattern of response for the majority of his life. His successfully developed survival instinct has blinded him to the actions he has justified to survive.

Slobodan Milosevic remains discretely behind the scenes. His game is much the same as the one he played before.

Radomir Diklic explains Milosevic's tactics this way: "Today, Milosevic has found someone else to take the fall for his Kosovo policy, the President of Serbia Milan Mlutinovic and the Serbian Government. In Catia , he proclaimed, "Its not me; it's the army." In Bosnia, he played at u reprimanding Karadzic for his actions. It is iron undertaking the role of umpire between the international community and his allies that he makes himself useful." As we all recall, this is a dangerous game."

Milosevic s Game HELENE DESPIC-POPOVIC
Liberation Paris, March 13

Milosevic's self-concept is such that he sees himself as a benevolent leader, loyal, determined and willing to fight for the rights of his people who he feels are unjustly being attacked by an overwhelming sinister force. He calls it NATO. His self-concept also has him believing that he is open to reasonable negotiation. However, it is his definition of reasonable and negotiable that causes NATO to feel that military action is the only form of communication that he understands.

"The international community's latest maneuvers have brought it into a position that is structurally no different from the one Milosevic has always held in public. The Serbian strongman has consistently maintained that Kosovo is simply another part of Serbia, and that the province's Albanian majority of almost 2 million – which has been boycotting the Serbian political system since 1990 – could start exercising its legitimate rights whenever it wanted.

"[If there are] some problems bothering them, Ratko Markovic, Milosevic's chief negotiator for Kosovo, has declared, they can always come and talk to the authorities of their country."

"Yet over the last six years, Milosevic never offered the Kosovo Albanians anything more than that status quo, nor is he likely to give them substantially more now, even if pressured by the Americans. Whatever else Milosevic may be, he is not a fool. He knows that keeping Kosovo within Serbia under any status is unsustainable in the long run. He is even more aware that he cannot survive politically if he loses Kosovo. Partition is an obvious solution for a man who has unsuccessfully tried to carve out a part of Croatia and succeeded in de facto partitioning Bosnia."

Transitions of October 1998, a monthly magazine about Central and Eastern Europe and the former Soviet Union (http://www.ijt.cz).

Milosevic, although achieving positions of power prior to having been elected President, has an unconscious self-concept, which suggests he feels inadequate and is compensating for these feelings with a reaction formation. That is, when someone says he is bad or wrong, he denies the feedback and asserts the correctness of his view regardless of its accuracy. Other peoples' accusations about his inappropriate behavior are seen as proof of the correctness of his behavior. The fundamental old decision in his character is that negative feedback means little because he believes most people don't understand his big picture of the way things ought to be.

"There are many historic causes for the hatred and instability that have consumed the Balkans for most of this century. But there's also general agreement among western historians and diplomats that it was Slobodan Milosevic who unleashed the current wave of nationalism and ethnic violence – exactly 11 years ago. It was then, in April 1987, that Yugoslavia's communist leadership in Belgrade sent Milosevic to Kosovo, a remote mountainous region where the Serbian Orthodox Church had its beginnings. Serbs call Kosovo their Jerusalem, and it was there in Kosovo that Milosevic re-ignited religious and nationalist passion throughout the Balkans when he threatened reprisals against Kosovo's Albanian majority. Virtually overnight, Milosevic became a hero to the Serbs, and six months later their president. It's a job he's held in one form or another ever since."

Charles Krause: "Today, a decade later, his critics in the United States and elsewhere say Milosevic is responsible for most of the carnage and war crimes committed in the Balkans. They also say he's become a dictator whose only real interest is to retain his personal power. The view that there's been a double standard is repeated daily on Serbia's state television and other government-controlled media, according to independent journalist Teofil Pancic."

Charles Ingrao: "He is totally dedicated to his own personal advancement and survival. I think he's extremely, totally immoral."

Teofil Pancic: "Milosevic builds a kind of xenophobic culture. We have a very xenophobic media, with a few exceptions. But most of the media are very xenophobic. And when you persuade your people that they are jeopardized from the outside world, then they will say, "Okay, if America says that Milosevic is no good, or somebody else, then Milosevic has to be good."

Charles Krause: "Louis Sell says the half truths and distortions appear not only in Yugoslavia's state-controlled media. He says they're also reflected in Milosevic's dealings with the United States and other foreign governments.

Charles Krause: Charles Ingrao is a professor of history at Purdue University who's written extensively on central Europe."

Outline newsHour Kosovo MacNeil-Lehrer
This NewsHour broadcast September 23, 1998

It seems impossible to believe that we end a millennium with behavior and actions so outrageous. Hitler's genocide and his skillful ability to enlist others into his pathological vision of the world are still today something we all grapple to believe and understand.

Sadam Hussein, Milosevic, Pol Pot, were not monsters who sprang from nowhere. They were people whose early life stories led to the logical conclusion of their behavior. Outrageous as it is, we must understand the origins that lead to extremes. Some might say that the fact that one had problems in his early childhood doesn't make him a Milosevic or a Hitler. This, of course, is true. I have looked at times at weeds, which grew out of cracks in buildings, and wondered how they got so high and how they managed to survive.

I suppose the answer is luck, timing, tenacity and the basic will to thrive.

Final thoughts after the air strikes ended – What will happen now? Here is how I see it.

- The mission statement remains the same, for the moment.
- The statement will change as other conflicts create pressure for similar action.
- World bodies, i.e., EU, UN and NATO are being redefined to respond to a "new" set of social values, based on increased communications, changing demographics and global economic ties.
- The stated mission statements from these organisations.
- The established mission statements of NATO and other world bodies will eventually lead to more human rights equality and more interventions economic, politically or militarily.
- Human rights will be the next millenium "tar baby" surfacing old debates, incriminations and misperceptions of historical events.

There will be increasing contention, conflict and subsequent crises.

To the NATO of 2000 and beyond, there will not just be a "tar baby"; there will be a world watching with live pictures of leader's struggling for clarity, communication and justice in an increasingly dangerous and yet shrinking global environment.

EPILOGUE

The foundations of The Goodfield method are rooted solidly in scientific principle. In 1980, at the First World Medical Energy Congress in Paris, I coined the term Scientific Humanism to describe my life's work. Today it is more apt than ever.

The humanistic assumptions about the underlying character of the person reflect my beliefs and experiences. To me, there need not be a mystical series of explanations to provide insight into our actions. As our days are often filled with data that seem to suggest that we have learned little in our evolution, I remained firmly convinced about our humanity. Convoluted thoughts and crazy actions may make good television, but it does not reveal the true picture.

As we enter into a new millennium, we bring with us our old prejudices, fears and fantasies about ourselves and others. Many are understandable; most are correctable; all can be overcome. S. I. Hayakawa wrote, more than thirty years ago, in an article we co-authored:

". . . but the general semanticist's belief, "communication is possible," also acts as a self-fulfilling prophecy."

Goodfield simply refused to take anyone's word for it that communication was impossible. So, to police officers and red-hot militants and everyone else, he kept putting the question, "Okay, if you are willing to communicate, when are you going to start?" (Hayakawa and Goodfield).

Here I am, three decades later, still asking, "When are you going to start?"

The key to the genuine communication, be it intra-psychic, inter-personal or on the international level, begins with the assumption that communication is possible. This assumption is at the heart of true change and growth.

There is one sentence that everyone will agree upon. Change is necessary. It is the next question that causes the trouble. Who, how, when? The answer to this question is usually: You, my way, now! If the leader is going to guide and not drag his followers into the next millennium, then it will be accomplished with the assumption that change is truly possible, and we can accomplish it together.

My definition of love and friendship is the same. It is when two big people are bigger together than when they are apart. This concept, of course, can be applied on both personal and professional levels. Being bigger together is a decision and a feeling that can only exist in the now.

What I have presented here is that victory in most all of life's endeavors requires preparation, training, determination and willingness to pay more than the next person. This is what prominent leaders, be they in the public or private sector, know and do. It is my sincere hope that these ideas and approaches may help in these important efforts and reduce the price paid while increasing the benefits.

Every tool or technique presented has been offered with one goal and one assumption. It is always possible to make a good system better; and deep substantive change need not take forever. It takes insight and action now.

All here is yours. One word of caution: As you change the world around you, you change the world within. That will change your life. Okay, if you are willing to change and take actions on what I have written, when are you going to start?

THE AUTHOR

Barry Austin Goodfield, director of the Goodfield Institute in San Anselmo, California, has practiced psychotherapy for 30 years, with a focus on analyzing nonverbal behavior. He has trained leaders of governments in conflict resolution and consults frequently for international organizations. Dr. Goodfield is Visiting Professor of Crisis Management and Conflict Resolution at the Diplomatic Academy of London, University of Westminster.

GLOSSARY

Body non-verbal leak (BNVL):
> The total body movement response as seen on an unconscious level.

Here and now:
> Living in the present and making decisions in relation to present factors.

Historical interactive non-verbal leak (HINVL):
> A perceived traumatic event that has as its origin a situation that occurred to a parent, grand parent or a family member that was passed down to a person in the present via an NVL, that resulted in a strategy that is counter-productive now.

Interactive non-verbal leak (INVL):
> A perceived traumatic event that results in an NVL. When that individual finds himself in a relationship, his NVL interacts with that of the other person with whom he is involved. It keeps both people together in a relationship, that I call compatible pathology as both are trying to work through their own PTEs.

Non-verbal leak (NVL):
> The non-verbal leak (NVL) is an often extraordinarily rapid, repetitive, patterned series of movements from the shoulders up, reflecting an unresolved perceived trauma and manifesting a decision and a strategy from the past, a decision and strategy believed to have been appropriate at the time, but that is maladaptive here and now.

PTE: Perceived traumatic event
> It is usually associated with a situation that occurred in childhood. It is an unconscious way of seeking balance, and protecting the person from experiencing pain. When a similar situation to the PTE arises again the old decision, now a new strategy, is there to protect the person.

> The result is a decision and then a strategy that is inconsistant with the needs and the demands of the environment now.

SOLUTION TO THE 9 DOT PROBLEM

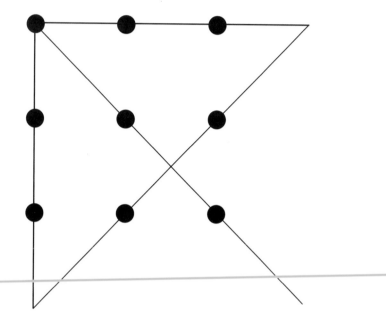

REFERENCES

Agrios, J.A. & Huberman, *The Presiding Judges Guide to Alternative Dispute Resolution.* A handbook for Canadian Judges on ADR in the Courts, An Electronic Book version 1.3 2, April 30, 1997.

Albright: *The Role of United States in Central Europe,* The Academy of Political Science, vol.38 no.1991.

Alvarez, A. *The Biggest Game in Town.* Boston: Houghton Mifflin. 1983.

Ayad, N. *The Information Explosion: A Challenge for Diplomacy.* Speech to Symposium Diplomacy beyond 2000. April 11, 1987.

Azar, E.E. *The Management of Protracted Social Conflict: Theory and Cases.* Hampshire, England: Gower. 1990.

Bratton, eds. *Governance and Politics in Africa,* (Boulder, CO: Lynne Rienner Publishers. 1992.

Brill, A.A. *The Basic Writings of Sigmund Freud,* The Modern Library, Random House, New York. 1938 Quoting Freud, S. *Psychopathology of Everyday Life.*

Brzezinski: *Differentiated Containment,* Zbigniew Brzezinski, Brent S. Scrowcroft, and Richard Murphy, Foreign Affairs, May/June 1997.

Burton, J. *Resolving Deep-rooted Conflict: A Handbook.* Lanham, MD, University Press of America. 1987.

Burton, J. *Conflict: Resolution and Prevention.* New York: St. Martin's Press. 1990 Connor, W. (1994). *Ethnonationalism: The Quest for Understanding.* Princeton, NJ: Princeton University Press. 1994.

Davidson, R.J., Ekman, P., Saron, C., Senulis, J., & Friesen, W.J. *Emotional Expression and Brain Physiology.*

Despic-Popovic, Helene, *Milosevic's Game,* Liberation Paris, March 13.

Deutch, John, former CIA Director, *Predictions for the 21st Century,* Council on Foreign relations Aug. 11,1997.

Ekman, P., Friesen, W.V. and Ancoli *Facial Signs of Emotional Experience.* Journal of Personality and Social Psychology, 39, pp. 1125-1134. 1980.

Ekman, P. and Friesen, W.V. *Hand Movements.* Journal of Communication, 22, pp. 353-374. 1972.

Ekman, P. *Telling Lies: Clues to Deceit in the Marketplace, Politics, and Marriage.* W.W.Norton & Company, New York & London 1992.

Ekman. P. *Mistakes When Deceiving.* Paper presented at the conference on the Clever Hands Phenomenon, New York Academy of Sciences, New York. 1980.

Ekman, P., Sorenson, E.R. and Friesen, W.V. *Pan-Cultural Elements in Facial Displays of Emotion.* Science, Vol. 164, No.3875, April 4, 1969.

NOTE: For comparison emblems in different cultures, see Ekman, *Movement with Precise Meanings,* Journal of Communication 26, pp. 14-26. 1976.

Gec, Jovana, Associated Press, Oct. 1996, Belgrade, Yugoslavia (AP).

Goertz, G. & Diehl, P.F. *Enduring Rivalries: Theoretical Constructs and Empirical Patterns.* International Studies Quarterly, 37, pp. 147-171. 1993.

Goldman-Eisler, F. *Psycholinguistics: Experiments in Spontaneous Speech.* New York: Academic Press. 1968.

Goodfield, B. A. and Norman, H. G. Wm. Deborah L. Jacobs, Editor, CPR Publications, Institute for Dispute Resolution, Vol. 12, No. 10, Oct. 1994.

Goodfield, B.A. and Norman, Wm. H.G. *A Truly Psychological Approach to Settlement,* Unpublished manuscript, 1991.

Gooyer de, G. F. *International Organized Crime.* Paper presented Vilnes Lithuania, Human Aspects of Crisis Management Seminar. 1994.

Hastie, R. *Causes and Effects of Causal Attribution.* Journal of Personality and Social Psychology, 46, 44-56. 1984.

Hastie, R. and Park, B. This chapter originally appeared in Psychological Review 93 (3), pp. 258 – 268. 1986.

Hastie, R. & Kumar, A.P. *Person Memory: Personality Traits as Organizing Principles in Memory for Behavior.* 1979.

Hayakawa, S.I. & Goodfield, B.A. *Reflections on a Visit to Watts*, vol.3, XXIII ETC. A Review of General Semantics. Psychology, 25, 37-38. Sept., 1996.

Julius Fast *Body Language*, M. Evens and Co. Inc. New York, 1970. The author describes a study done by Ekman, Sorenson and Friesen, Science,Vol.164, No.3875, April 4, 1969.

Kahneman, D. (1973), *Attention and Effort.* Englewood Cliffs, NJ: Prentice-Hall Lannin: Byline: by Patrick Lannin, Reuter News Service-CIS and Eastern Europe, Jan. 11, 1996.

Levenson, R.W., Ekman, P. & Friesen, W.V. *Voluntary Facial Activity Generates Emotion-specific Autonomic Nervous System Activity.* Psychophysiology, 27, pp. 363-384. 1990.

Keyes, R. *Changing It.* Boston: Little, Brown. 1985.

Kraut, R.E. *Humans As Lie Detectors: Some Second Thoughts.* Journal of Communications, 30, 209-216. 1980.

Kriesberg, L. *Intractable Conflicts.* Peace Review, 5, 417-421. 1993.

Lemarchand, Rene *Africa's Troubled Transitions*, Journal of Democracy 3 (October 1993): 98-109.

Lykken, D.T. *The Detection of Deception.* Psychological Bulletin, 86, pp. 47-53. 1979.

MacNeil-Lehrer, Outline News Hour Kosovo. This News Hour broadcast September 23, 1998.

Mehrabian, A. *Nonverbal Betrayal of Feeling.* Journal of Experimental Research in Personality, 5, 64-73. 1971.

Mitroff, I.I. & Pearson, C.M. *Crisis Management: A Diagnostic Guide for Improving Your Organization's Crisis-preparedness.* Jossey-Bass Publishers, San Francisco. 1993.

Pemberton, W.H. *Sanity for Survival: A Semantic Approach to Conflict Resolution.* Pemberton Publications, 3rd edition, p. 162. 1989.

Robertson: The Academy of Political Science Proceedings, Vol. 38, no.1, p.1740. 1991.

Rosenblum, Mort *Squandering Eden: Africa at the Edge,* with Doug Williamson.

Rosenblum, Mort *Who stole the news?* John Wiley & Sons, Inc., New York, 1993.

Rouhana, N.N. *Unofficial Intervention: Potential Contributions to Resolving* International Conflicts. In J. Melissen (Ed.), Innovations in Diplomatic Practice, pp. 111-132. Asingstoke, England: Macmillan. 1998.

Rubin, J.Z., Pruitt, D. and Kim S. *Social Conflict.* New York: McGraw-Hill. 1994.

Sjoberg, L. *Risk Perception: Experts and the Public.* European Psychologist, Volume 3/1, Hogrefe & Huber Publishers. 1998.

Sjoberg, L & af Wahlberg, A. (1996). *Sandsjoolyckan.* (Rhizikon: Rapport fran Centrum for Riskforskning No.6). Stockholm: Centrum for Riskforskning.

Sjoberg, L., af Wahlberg, A. and Kvist, P. (In press). *The Rise of Risk: Risk Related Bills Submitted to the Swedish Parliament in 1964/65 and 1993/95.* Journal of Risk Research.

Smith, S. *A Comparative Analysis of Neuro-linguistic Programming and the Goodfield Method.* Basic Training paper, 1994.

Spiegel, D. The Harvard Mental Health Letter, Sept. 1998.

Srull, T.K. *Person Memory: Some Tests of Associative Storage and Retrieval Models.* Journal of Experimental Psychology: Human Learning and Memory, 7, 440-463. 1981.

Thackrey, T. *Gambling Secrets of Nick the Greek.* Chicago: Rand McNally. 1968.

Tomkins, S.S., *Affect, Imagery, Unconsciousness: Vol.1.* New York: Springer. 1962.

Transitions of October 1998, a monthly magazine about Central and Eastern Europe and the former Soviet Union.

Tversky, A. & Kahneman, D. *Availability: A Heuristic for Judging Frequency and Probability.* Cognitive Psychology, 4, pp. 207-232. 1973.

Tversky, A. & Kahneman, D. *Judgement Under Uncertainty: Heuristics and Biases* Science, 185, 1124-1131. 1974.

Verbruggen, L. Executive Secretary of Nato (Nato's goals).

INDEX